NEW

Grammar Time

5

PEARSON
Longman

Sandy Jervis

Pearson Education Limited
Edinburgh Gate
Harlow
Essex CM20 2JE
England
and Associated Companies throughout the World.

www.longman.com

© Pearson Education Limited 2008

First published 2001
This edition 2008
Second impression 2009

Student Book ISBN: 978-1-4058-5278-4
Multi-Rom ISBN: 978-1-4058-5277-7
Pack ISBN: 978-1-4058-6701-6

Printed and bound in Italy by G. Canale & C. S.p.A
Cover by Mackerel Design, illustrations by Kate Shannon
Designed and Project Managed by Starfish Design
Editorial and Project Management Ltd.

Contents

Present tenses (1)

Present simple, present continuous, state verbs

(Picture 1) Hi, guys, listen to this ....

Beth: It sounds awful!
Lucy: I hate it! It's just a horrible racket!
Peter: I love it! Who's playing the guitar? I think he's great!

(Picture 2) I am. Thanks! I'm Dash, Harry's cousin.

Harry: Dash is staying with us for a few weeks. He's got a new job in London and he's looking for a flat.
Peter: Great! What do you do, Dash?
Dash: I'm a music teacher.
Harry: He's in a band, too! They're making their first CD! Listen to this!
Beth: Well, it doesn't sound that bad …
Lucy: No, not at all. Actually …

(Picture 3) It's OK!

1 Complete the tables.

Present simple

Positive	I / You / We / They	live	
	He / She / It	....	
Negative	I / You / We / They	.... not (don't)	live
	He / She / It	does not	
Questions	Do	I / you / we / they	live?
	Does	he / she / it	

Present continuous

Positive	I	.... ('m)	looking
	He / She / It	is	
	We / You / They	.... ('re)	
Negative	I	am not	looking
	He / She / It	.... (isn't)	
	We / You / They	are not	
Questions	Am	I	
	Is	he / she / it	.... ?
	Are	you / we / they	

2 **Read the information.**

Present simple

Use

We use the present simple to talk about
* habits, repeated actions or something we do regularly

I usually watch TV after dinner.
He plays the guitar in a band.
* facts, things that are always or usually true

Chris lives in Scotland.   Hens lay eggs.
* programmes and timetables

Our train leaves at 8.30 a.m.
The film starts at 6 o'clock.

Time expressions

We use these expressions with the present simple. Their place is at the beginning or the end of the sentence.
* *in (January), in the morning / the afternoon / the evening*

The shop closes for a few days in August.
In the afternoon, I sit in the garden and have a cup of tea.
* *on (Mondays / Monday), on weekdays, on (Saturday) morning / afternoon / evening*
* *at the weekend*

We don't go to school on Sunday.
On Tuesday afternoon, I go to an art class.
* *every day / week / month, once / twice / three times (etc) a week / month / year*

I drink two glasses of milk every day.
They go on holiday twice a year.

Adverbs of frequency

We use adverbs of frequency to show how often we do something. Usually, their place is before the main verb or after the verb *be*.
* *always, usually, often, sometimes, never*

My sister sometimes borrows my clothes.
Do they usually stay up late?
I'm always hungry.
This door is never closed.

Present continuous

Use

We use the present continuous to talk about
* something that is happening now (at the moment or for a longer period).

Mum is talking on the phone right now.
He's taking driving lessons this month.
* temporary situations, something that is happening this time only

I'm staying at my grandmother's for a few days.
She usually takes the bus to school, but today she's walking.

Time expressions

We use these time expressions with the present continuous. Their place is at the beginning or the end of the sentence
* *at the moment, now, right now, today, this week / month / year, these days*

It isn't raining at the moment.
He's working hard these days.

3 **Complete with the present simple.**

1 My dad usually ...*drives*... to work. (drive)
2 Their plane .... at 9 a.m. (leave)
3 We .... meat every day. (not eat)
4 What time .... they ....? (get up)

5 I never .... this computer. (use)
6 I'm a musician. What .... you ....? (do)
7 She .... coffee. (not drink)

4 **Complete with the present continuous.**

1 I can't go out. ...*I'm doing*... my homework. (do)
2 Sandra .... jeans today. (not wear)
3 .... your cousin .... with you these days? (live)

4 Sorry, ... you .... to me? (talk)
5 What .... they .... here? (do)
6 Ethan and I .... the match on TV. (watch)
7 He .... very fast. (not run)

5 **Match.**

1 He plays the piano.   happening now
    He's playing the piano.   fact

2 They're staying at a hotel.   temporary
    They often stay at a hotel.   repeated action

3 I always have cereal for breakfast.   this time only
    I'm having cereal for breakfast today.   habit

4 The sun is setting. Isn't it beautiful?   happening now
    The sun sets in the West.   fact

5 The film starts at 10 o'clock.   happening now
    Shh! The film is starting!   programme

6 **Circle the correct answer.**

1 Can I call you back? We have / **are having** lunch at the moment.
2 Elizabeth doesn't eat / isn't eating red meat. She's a vegetarian.
3 What do you do / are you doing right now?
4 We don't watch / aren't watching TV in the morning.
5 She wants to live in Brighton but she lives / is living in London at the moment.
6 I don't cook / 'm not cooking today. There are sandwiches in the fridge.
7 Do they look / Are they looking for a new car?
8 The match usually finishes / is finishing at 8 o'clock.
9 Look! The red hen lays / is laying an egg!
10 We don't usually listen / aren't usually listening to this kind of music.

7 **Complete with the present simple or the present continuous.**

1 I _get up_ at 7 o'clock on weekdays. (get up)
2 Hurry up! John .... for you outside the cinema. (wait)
3 What .... you usually .... at the weekends? (do)
4 Dad .... to the office today. It's a bank holiday. (not go)
5 .... they .... at the moment? (work)
6 We .... cake for breakfast every day. (not have)
7 .... she .... her grandparents every week? (visit)
8 They .... for their final exam at the moment. (study)
9 I .... to this radio show every week. (listen)
10 The sun .... today! (shine)

8 **Circle the correct answer.**

1 Alex is sleeping **at the moment** / every day.
2 Are you leaving right now / every weekend?
3 They practice every day / today.
4 We aren't staying at a hotel every year / this time.
5 Henry and I play football at the weekend / right now.
6 Is it raining every evening / at the moment?
7 Does she wash her hands today / before she starts cooking?
8 We do the shopping this month / on Saturdays.
9 The restaurant is doing a special deal on pizzas this week / every week: buy one, get one free!
10 This shop doesn't open right now / on Sundays.

9 **Choose and complete.**

Peter [1] *usually*........ walks to school, but [2]............... he's riding his
bike. [3]................, he has football practice after school and he doesn't
want to be late.
(on Mondays, usually, today)

It is 3 p.m. Beth is playing a computer game [4].................
She [5]................ reads a book, but she never watches TV [6].................
(sometimes, in the afternoon, at the moment)

[7]................, Lucy relaxes in her room. She [8]................ listens to
music or writes emails to her friends. [9]................, she's painting
Cosmo's portrait.
(often, Right now, on Sunday evening)

10 **Read and complete. Use the present simple or the present continuous.**

Chairman Chapman at work.

TeenLink

Interview of the week

Welcome to this year's first issue of *TeenLink* magazine.
This week our school is helping to reforest Belview Hill.
Beth Banks interviewed Martin Chapman, the chairman
of our local committee for the preservation of the environment.

Beth: You [1] *'re working*... (work) very hard today.
Martin: Yes, we are. We [2]................ (plant) more trees.
Beth: Why [3]................ (you / do) this?
Martin: Well, it usually [4]................ (rain) a lot in this area and the water
 [5]................ (carry) the soil away. We often [6]................ (have) floods.
 So we need more trees. Trees are important because their roots [7]................
 (keep) the soil in its place.
Beth: Who's helping you today?
Martin: A lot of local people. Some people [8]................ (dig) holes and others
 [9]................ (water) the trees. Many of your schoolmates [10]................
 (help), too, so we [11]................ (do) the work fast.
Beth: I often [12]................ (help) my dad in the garden. Is there anything I can do?

11 Read the information.

State verbs

Some verbs describe a state, not an action. These verbs do not have a continuous form. We use them only in the present simple form. These verbs are:

- *see, look, hear, sound, smell, taste, feel*
- *like, dislike, love, hate, prefer, not mind*
- *think, know, believe, seem, remember, forget, remind, understand, realise*
- *have (= possess), want, need, mean, own, belong, cost*

This music sounds horrible!
~~This music is sounding horrible!~~
I think he's very good.
~~I'm thinking he's very good.~~

Some state verbs can be both state and action verbs depending on their meaning. As state verbs they do not have a continuous form, but as action verbs they do. Look at these examples:

- *She has her MP3 player with her today.*
  (have = possess, state verb)
- *She's having lunch with her friends today.*
  (have lunch = eat, action verb)
- *I think you're right.*
  (think = believe, have an opinion, state verb)
- *What are you thinking about?* (think = what goes through our mind, active verb)

Other verbs like these are:

State verb	Action verb
see	see (= meet)
look (= appear)	look
smell (= have an odour)	smell
feel (= have texture)	feel (= give an impression)

12 Cross out the wrong sentence.

1 ~~Is this perfume smelling nice?~~
   Does this perfume smell nice?

2 She has two cats and a goldfish.
   She's having two cats and a goldfish.

3 I'm thinking it's a good idea.
   I think it's a good idea!

4 This book looks very old.
   This book is looking very old.

5 Why do you smell the cheese? Is it off?
   Why are you smelling the cheese? Is it off?

6 Harry can't come to the phone. He's having a shower.
   Harry can't come to the phone. He has a shower.

7 Why are you looking at me like that? Is there something on my face?
   Why do you look at me like that? Is there something on my face?

8 I don't know what to do. I'm thinking about it.
   I don't know what to do. I think about it.

13 Complete with the present simple or the present continuous.

1 Their new CD is great! What ...*do*........... you ...*think*........... ? (think)

2 There's Jenny! She .... at us! (wave)

3 I .... his story. I .... he's lying. (not believe, think)

4 .... you .... your first toy? (remember)

5 She .... blue cheese. She never eats it. (hate)

6 I'm not sure I can buy this bike. I .... it's too expensive. (think)

7 .... this bag .... to Pam? (belong)

8 Paul .... very cheerful these days. (not seem)

9 Timothy .... a music lesson at the moment. (have)

10 They .... a word! They can't speak our language. (not understand)

11 You can go out with your friends. I .... ! (not mind)

12 What .... this word .... ? (mean)

14 **Read and choose the correct answer.**

TeenLink

Hello! My name's Beth Banks. ¹ _Do you remember_ me?
I ² .... this note to introduce myself and my friends to our new readers: I'm twelve
years old and I ³ .... to the same school as Harry, Peter and Lucy.

Harry Davis is the Editor of the school magazine, *TeenLink*. He ⁴ .... what goes
into the magazine. He's a good friend and he ⁵ .... something good about my work;
I usually take photos and ⁶ .... some of the articles. But these days, I ⁷ ....
for an important French exam, so I ⁸ .... much time for the magazine.

Peter Hardy is fourteen years old and he's in the same class as Harry. He ⁹ .... jokes
and food! He's with me at the moment: he ¹⁰ .... his third ice cream!

Lucy is Peter's sister. She's only eleven but she's got a great talent: she ¹¹ .... like a
real artist! At the moment, she ¹² .... the violin. Unfortunately, she hasn't got any
talent for music!

1 a You remember	b Are you remembering	c Do you remember
2 a write	b am writing	c writing
3 a 'm going	b goes	c go
4 a decides	b is deciding	c does decide
5 a always says	b says always	c is always saying
6 a writes	b writing	c write
7 a study	b am studying	c studying
8 a not have	b don't have	c hasn't
9 a loves	b love	c is loving
10 a eat	b eats	c is eating
11 a paint	b is painting	c paints
12 a plays	b is playing	c play

15 **Write about you, your friends and / or family.**

Write about what you usually do, how you spend your time, your likes and dislikes.
Write about what you are doing at the moment, or these days.

....
....
....
....
....
....

2 Past tenses (1)

Past simple, 'used to', past continuous

I'm sorry, Nick!

TeenLink

Sports Shorts
by Harry Davis

Matt Taylor, the well-known basketball player, got a nasty shock during the basketball game last Friday. He was trying to steal the ball from Ricky Fitz, a player for the other team, when a gigantic St Bernard's dog jumped on him, threw him to the ground and held him down with his huge paws. All the players tried to help, but the dog didn't move. However, when Ricky Fitz ordered the dog to get off the court, it left immediately! After the game, Ricky explained. 'That was my dog, Bernie. He used to be a police dog. In his mind, when he jumped on poor Matt, he was attacking a nasty thief!'

Our school football team played against Berkeley Comprehensive yesterday at …

---

1 **Complete the tables.**

Past simple

Positive	
Regular verbs	
I / You / He / She / It / We / They	jumped order………
Irregular Verbs	
I / You / He / She / It / We / They	left held

Negative	
Regular verbs	
I / You / He / She / It / We / They	……………… (didn't) jump
Irregular Verbs	
I / You / He / She / It / We / They	did not (…………….) leave

Question		
Regular / Irregular verbs		
Did	I / you / he / she / it / we / you / they	order?

Used to

Positive			Negative			
Regular and irregular verbs			**Regular and irregular verbs**			
I / You / He / She / It / We / You / They	used to	play be	I / You / He / She / It / We / You / They	did not (...............)	use to	be

Question			
Regular and irregular verbs			
Did	I / you / he / she / it / we / you / they	use to	play? .... ?

Past continuous

Positive			Negative		
Regular and irregular verbs			**Regular and irregular verbs**		
I / You / He / She / It	was	trying	I / You / He / She / It	was not (................)	try ....
We / You / They	were	throw	We / You / They	................(weren't)	throwing

Question		
Was	I / you / he / she / it	................?
Were	we / you /they	throwing ... ?

2 **Read the information.**

Past simple

Use

We use the past simple to talk about

• an action that started and finished in the past. We usually say when it happened or imply that it was a specific time in the past.

They went to Spain last year.

• a past state

We lived in London in 2001.

• a past habit

He exercised every day when he was at college.

Form

• To form the past simple of regular verbs, we add -ed or -d to the main verb.

jump → jumped   try → tried

stop → stopped love → loved

• Irregular verbs don't form the past simple with -ed. Each irregular verb is different.

go → went   get → got   take → took

leave → left

• In negative sentences and questions, we use did / didn't and the infinitive. We don't use the past simple form of the verb.

She didn't answer the phone.

~~She didn't answered the phone.~~

Did they break the vase?

~~Did they broke the vase?~~

• The past simple of be is was / were. Remember: we don't use did / didn't with was / were.

He was a good student.

We weren't cold last night.

Time expressions

We use these time expressions with the past simple:

• *yesterday, yesterday morning / afternoon / evening*

• *this morning / afternoon (when they are in the past)*

• *two hours / days / weeks / months / years ago*

• *last week / month / year / Saturday night*

• *in 2008 / June / the summer*

Used to

Use

We use *used to* to talk about past habits or states that were true in the past, but are not true now.

• *I used to stay with my grandmother every summer when I was a child.*

11

3 Write sentences in the past simple.

1 *They didn't play football* last Saturday. *They went to the beach* .
(they / play / football ✗, they / go / to the beach ✓)

2 .... last night. .... (I / study ✗, I / listen / to music ✓)

3 .... at 3 a.m. last night. .... (He / wake up ✓, he / feel well. ✗)

4 .... because .... (She / buy / a camera ✗, she / have / the money ✗)

5 .... because .... (We / open / the letter ✗, it / be / for us ✓)

6 ...., but .... (They / drink / some lemonade ✓, they / eat / anything ✗)

7 .... so .... (He / do / his best ✗, he / win / the race ✗)

4 Ask the questions and complete the answers in the past simple.

1 **A:** When *did you see* .... Harry? (you / see)
B: Yesterday afternoon. He *gave* .... me this book for you. (give)

2 **A:** .... after midnight? (the film / finish)
B: I don't know. I .... TV last night. (not watch)

3 **A:** .... all the milk this morning? (your brothers / drink)
B: No, they .... There's some milk in this jug.

4 **A:** Where .... Adam? (she / meet)
B: She .... him at Martha's house, but he .... her.
(meet, not remember)

5 **A:** .... George to the party? (you / invite)
B: Yes, I .... I also .... his friend because
he .... nice. (invite, seem)

5 Rewrite the sentences with *used to*.

Read the secrets Mrs Banks wrote in her diary when she was eight years old.

My secrets

1 My best friend is Olivia. She's got long, red hair and green eyes. We go everywhere together.
2 There's fish for dinner twice a week. I don't like fish!
3 Our teacher doesn't give us a lot of homework. I finish early and play with my dolls.
4 I don't tidy my room very often. I have more important things to do!
5 Mum hides the biscuit jar in different places. I find it every time!

Now write what she says to her daughter, Beth.

1 *When I was eight, my best friend used to be Olivia. She used to ...*
....

2 ....
....

3 ....
....

4 ....
....

5 ....
....

6   **Read the information.**

Past continuous

We use the past continuous to talk about

- an action that was in progress at a specific time in the past.

I was doing my homework at 6.30 p.m.
They were driving to work at that time.

- two actions that were in progress at the same time in the past. We use *while* to link the two sentences.

I was reading a magazine while the boys were playing in the garden.
While he was talking on the phone, she was drying her hair.

Past simple and past continuous

- We use the past simple and past continuous to talk about an action that happened (past simple) while another action was in progress (past continuous).

We were having lunch when we heard a loud bang.

- To link the sentences, we use *when* before the past simple and *while* or *as* before the past continuous.

It was raining when we came out of the cinema.
When the teacher came in, we were sitting down.
As she was looking through her papers, she found my diary.

7   **Complete with the past continuous.**

What was everyone doing at 8.00 p.m. yesterday evening?

1   Peter ...was studying............... for a test. (study)
2   Lucy .... an email to her pen friend. (write)
3   Mr and Mrs Hardy .... TV. (watch)
4   Harry .... a shower. (have)
5   Beth and her cousin .... a computer game. (play)
6   I .... to my friend on the phone. (talk)
7   You .... to London. (fly)
8   Mrs Jones .... her pupil's homework. (mark)

> **Look!**
>
> When you begin with 'while', remember to add a comma at the end of the clause.

8   **Join the sentences with *while*.**

1   (while) we / play / football they / have / a lesson ...While we were playing football, they were having a lesson..
2   he / listen/ to music (while) he / run ....
3   (while) they / paint / the chairs Tom / plant / the new trees ....
4   Mary / make / the tea (while) Ken / make / the sandwiches ....
5   (while) Dad / fish we / swimming / in the sea...
6   I / do / the crossword (while) you / play / computer games ....

9   **Circle the correct answer.**

1   As I was taking / took the shoes to the till, I was realising / realised I did not have any money with me.
2   The doorbell was ringing / rang while they were watching / watched TV.
3   While we were talking / talked, the baby was waking up / woke up.
4   David was cycling / cycled home when it was starting / started to rain.
5   I was hurting / hurt my back as I was lifting / lifted a heavy box.
6   Elizabeth was driving / drove to work when the accident was happening / happened.
7   While they weren't looking / didn't look, someone was stealing / stole their luggage.
8   The train was leaving / left while you were buying / bought the magazines.

2

(10) **Complete with the past simple or the past continuous.**

1 I *was locking* (lock) the front door when the phone *rang* . (ring)
2 .... William .... (talk) to anyone while he .... ? (wait)
3 We .... (work) for the same company when we .... (meet)
4 The speaker .... (say) something important while you ....
   (not listen)
5 Liz .... (lose) her glasses as she .... (run) in the park.
6 .... they .... (go) home when you .... (see) them?
7 John .... (play) the guitar when I .... (walk) into the room.
8 When I .... (leave), the boys .... (listen) to music.

(11) **Join the sentences.**

1 Mrs Hardy / talk / on the phone. Peter / got / home. (when)
   Mrs Hardy was talking on the phone when Peter got home. ....
2 Harry / fall asleep. He / watch / TV. (while) ....
3 The Headteacher / walk / in. We / do / a test. (while) ....
4 I / break / the plate. I / do / the washing up. (as) ....
5 She / get up. They / have / breakfast in the kitchen. (when) ....
6 It / start / to snow. They / climb / the mountain. (as) ....
7 I / get on / the plane. Someone / shout / my name. (when) ....
8 The children / take / this photo of you. You / sleep. (while) ....

(12) **Complete with the past simple or the past continuous.**

Peter: Here's my album of funny photos!
Leo: Look at this photo of Lucy!
Peter: Yes, she ¹ *was smiling* (smile) for the camera when the bee ² *stung* (sting) her on the nose!
Leo: Poor Lucy! What about this?
Peter: That's Harry on his new bike when he was eight. He ³ .... (not look) when he
        ⁴ .... (hit) that tree! I ⁵ .... (not have) time to warn him.
Leo: Oh, no! You've got my photograph, too!
Peter: Oh, yes. What were you doing?
Leo: I ⁶ .... (watch) the football game on TV when you ⁷ .... (shout) next to my ear!
Peter: That's Beth. She ⁸ .... (drinking) strawberry juice at my last birthday party when
        someone ⁹ .... (push) her. She ¹⁰ .... (spill) it all over her new white dress!
Lucy: What about this photo from your party, then?
Peter: Where ¹¹ .... (you / find) it? Give it to me!
Lucy: Peter ¹² .... (blow out) his candles when he ¹³ .... (slip) and ¹⁴ .... (fall)
        face down onto his birthday cake! That was really funny!

13 Complete with the past simple or past continuous.

TeenLink

Most embarrassing!

This week we asked Mr Irons, our PE teacher, about his most embarrassing moment. Enjoy the answer!

Ten years ago, my brother was in his last year at Art school. He 1 _was taking_ (take) part in a young artists' competition with a big piece of sculpture. He called it 'War'. I 2 .... (not know) anything about modern art then and, to me, it 3 .... (look) like a pile of old metal pieces.

On the day of the competition, my brother 4 .... (decide) to put his piece of sculpture in a different place. He asked me and a friend to help him and then he 5 .... (go) to get something from the car. Unfortunately, while we 6 .... (carry) the thing to its new place, I 7 .... (slip) and 8 .... (fall). When I 9 .... (get) up, all the metal pieces etc 10 .... (lie) all over the floor!

14 Complete with *one* word.

I was so shocked that I didn't know what to do! Then, my friend had an idea.

'Why don't we just put everything back? Who will know the difference?'

So, while the judges 1 .... looking at the other works of art, my friend and I put everything back together again. We simply 2 .... everything back into a pile and decided that it 3 .... look bad! We were 4 .... the last piece on the top when the judges arrived together with my brother. 5 .... he saw the state of his work, his face became white with anger and mine red with embarrassment! 6 .... the judges were examining the sculpture, he 7 .... to me: 'I'll kill you for this!' The only reason I am here today to tell the story is because the judges really liked his work – or should I say our work? Actually, they 8 .... it was so good that they gave him the 1st prize!

Writing practice

15 Write to *TeenLink*.

Write about your funniest, most exciting or most embarrassing moment (between 60–80 words).

When was it? Where were you and with whom?
What were you doing when it happened? How did people react?

....
....
....
....
....

Present tenses (2)

Present perfect simple, present perfect continuous

Just a thought ... from the editor

I've been looking through some old photos just now and I've found one that dates back to 1982. It's a photo of my parents, on their way to a party, on the last day of school. My parents have known each other since primary school and have been married for eighteen years. The two young people have changed quite a lot since then – Dad's lost most of his hair, for a start! Back in 1982, as I see in the photo, Dad had to carry his stack of heavy vinyl LP records from party to party – I can fit endless hours of music in one tiny MP3 player. We also have mobile phones, high-speed Internet and digital cameras.

Yes, many things have changed, but, on the other hand, have you ever thought about how some things have stayed the same? If I look at the photo more closely, in the background, I can see Mr Thomson's bakery. Everyone in my family loves his famous teacakes and he's been making them since 1957. Next to the bakery, there's 'Bookworm', the bookshop. It first opened in 1906, so it has been doing business for more than a century!

I'd like to hear of more places like that. If you want to help, walk around our town and find out what hasn't changed at all in the last thirty years, or more. Send your emails to:

h-davis@teenlink.co.uk

Harry Davis

1 **Complete the table.**

Present perfect simple			
Positive	I / We / You / They He / She / It	have ('ve) has ('s)	changed.
Negative	I / We / You / They He / She / It	.... not (haven't) has not (...............)	changed.
Question	.... Has	I / we / you / they he / she / it	changed?

Present perfect continuous			
Positive	I / We / You / They He / She / It	have ('ve) has (...............)	been looking.
Negative	I / We / You / They He / She / It	have not (haven't) .... (hasn't)	been ....
Question	Have	I / we / you / they he / she / it	.... looking?

2 **Read the information.**

Use

We use the present perfect to talk about
- something that happened in the recent past and its results affect the present.

I've left my book at school. I can't do my homework now!
- something that happened in the past, but we do not mention when.

A new restaurant has opened near the cinema.
- a state that began in the past and continues up to the present.

She's worked in this shop since 1997.
I've known him since we were four years old.
- our experiences, something we have or have not done.

We've been on a hot air balloon flight.
I've seen all his films.
- We often use *ever* and *never* with the present perfect when we talk about our experiences. We use *ever* in questions.

Have you ever done an extreme sport?
- We only use *never* in positive sentences. The meaning of a sentence with *never* is negative: *never* + positive verb = negative meaning.

We have never met. ✓
I haven't never played golf. ✗

Form

We use *have / has* and the past participle of the verb to form the present perfect.
We form the past participle of regular verbs by adding *-(e)d* to the infinitive.

look → *looked*   *change* → *changed*
travel → *travelled*

Irregular verbs do not follow a rule. Each verb has a different past participle.

make → *made*   *cut* → *cut*   *give* → *given*
teach → *taught*

Time markers

The time markers we use with the present perfect have different positions in the sentence.
Read the examples.

just	*They've just come back from school.*
yet	*Have they called yet?*
	We haven't finished yet.
for	*This shop has been here for ten years.*
since	*I haven't seen them since 2005.*
ever /	*Has it ever snowed in May?*
never	*She's never thought about it.*
so far	*So far, I've written three emails.*
	They haven't done anything so far.
recently /	*I've read an interesting book recently.*
lately	*It hasn't rained lately.*
always	*We've always liked your work.*

3 **Complete with the present perfect simple.**

1 I .....*'ve found*.............. some old photos of my parents. (find)

2 Ron .... Canada twice. (visit)

3 They .... the question. (not understand)

4 .... his presents yet? (he / open)

5 I'm sorry, we .... all the biscuits. (eat)

6 .... any good films lately? (you / see)

7 Diana .... Ian to the party. (not invite)

8 .... with the computer? I need to do some work. (the boys / finish)

9 She .... her phone number. (change)

10 I .... to the new CD yet. (not listen)

4 **Ask the questions and complete the answers.**

1 A: *Have you ever been to Australia?*   you / be / to Australia?   B: *No, I haven't*....

2 A: ....   they / see / a snake?   B: Yes, ...

3 A: ....   she / meet / someone famous?   B: No, ...

4 A: ....   he / ride a horse?   B: No, ...

5 A: ....   you / have / a toothache?   B: Yes, ...

6 A: ....   they / be / late before?   B: Yes, ...

3

5 **Choose and write. Use the present perfect.**

I / never / meet / him   just / leave   see / this film   ~~do / all the work~~
never / play / volley ball before   already / have / lunch   move / to Cornwall
not sleep / well / for three days

1 We *'ve done all the work* . You don't need to do anything.
2 Fred .... He doesn't live here any more.
3 I .... Let's go and see something else.
4 They aren't hungry because they ....
5 I'm afraid you can't see Mr Mason. He ....
6 He .... That's why he's so bad at it.
7 We .... and we are tired!
8 I .... so I don't know what he looks like.

6 **Circle the correct answer.**

1 She's (already)/ yet gone home.
2 We've had this car for / since 1998.
3 Have you finished your homework project just / yet?
4 I've known Angela for / since we were two years old.
5 Adrian has never / ever used the Internet!

6 We haven't had any news so far / already.
7 She hasn't spoken to me for / since last January.
8 I've just / yet painted these chairs, so be careful.
9 Have they never / ever used an electronic dictionary before?
10 Graham has always / so far drunk fruit juice for breakfast.

7 **Write dialogues.**

1 **A**: Peter / get up (yet)
   B: he / have breakfast (already)
   Has Peter got up yet?
   Yes , *he has already had breakfast* .
2 **A**: the children / come out (yet)
   B: the lesson / finish (just)
   ....
   No, ...
3 **A**: you / win / a competition (ever)
   B: I / enter / a competition (never)
   ....
   No, ...
4 **A**: Chris / know / Ethan (for a long time)
   B: they / meet (just)
   ....
   I think ....
5 **A**: they / be / busy at the shop (always)
   B: they /be / very busy (lately)
   ....
   No, but ....
6 **A**: Joe / move / into this house (recently)
   B: he / live / there (always)
   ....
   No, ...

8 **Rewrite the sentences.**

1 Mark has never ridden a bike before. It's the first time *Mike has ever ridden a bike* .
2 It's the third time I've read this book. I've read *this book three times* .
3 It's the first time we've ever been to a concert. We ....
4 They've never visited a museum before. It's ....
5 Sandra has travelled to the USA five times. It's the fifth time ....
6 You've never complained about the food before. It's the first time ....
7 It's the fourth time I've been to this adventure park. I've ....
8 It's the first time it has ever snowed here! It has ....

9 **Read the information.**

> **have been to and have gone to**
> The verb *go* has two forms in the present perfect: *have gone* and *have been*.
> Look at the two examples to see the difference in meaning.
>
> *She's been to the supermarket.*
> (She went there earlier and now she is back.)
> *She's gone to the supermarket.*
> (She went there earlier and she is still there.)

10 **Match.**

1 Look, Dennis has bought new clothes.   a He's gone to the shops.
   Dennis hasn't come back, yet.   b He's been to the shops.

2 Is Mary in her room?   a Yes, she's been to the cinema.
   Has Mary had a good time?   b No, she's gone to the cinema.

3 The boys aren't at home.   a They've gone to the gym.
   The boys have just come back.   b They've been to the gym.

4 Are Jenny and Fiona at work?   a No, they've gone on holiday.
   Jenny and Fiona look great, don't they?   b Yes, they've just been on holiday.

11 **Complete with *has / have gone* or *has / have been*.**

1 I 've............. never ..been........... to a tropical island.
2 Sue isn't at home. She .... to Brussels on business.
3 They .... to the farmers' market. They've bought lots of fresh fruit.
4 You've got a tan. .... you .... on holiday?
5 Nick .... for a walk. He'll be back in an hour.
6 Tania .... to her sister's. Would you like to call her there?
7 What are all these books? .... you .... to the library?
8 Mike .... into hospital. He's asked me to feed his cat while he's away.

12 **Read the information.**

> **Present perfect or past simple?**
> We use both the past simple and present perfect to talk about something that happened in the past. The difference is that
> • we use the past simple to talk about something that happened at a specific time in the past. We either say or imply exactly when it happened.
> • we use the present perfect to put emphasis on the fact that something has happened. We do not say when exactly it happened.
> • Compare the examples:
> *I bought this CD last week.*
> *They read this book when they were at school.*
> *I've bought a new CD.*
> *They've read this book.*
>
> • We use the present perfect to talk about our experiences to put emphasis on what we have / haven't done. When we ask specific questions or give specific details about them we use the past simple.
> *'Have you ever seen an elephant?'*
> *Yes, I have.'*
> *'Where did you see it?'*
> *'I saw it at London Zoo.'*
> *'Really? When did you go there?'*
> *'In 2007.'*

13 **Circle the correct answer.**

1 He's a well-known writer. He published / has published six books.

2 Kate answered / has answered the phone when I called.

3 We were very young when the accident happened / has happened.

4 Have you heard about John? He broke / 's broken his leg.

5 I love this band. I downloaded / have downloaded all their albums onto my MP3 player.

6 The last time we saw / have seen him was at Penny's birthday party.

7 I ate / have eaten all the crisps last night, sorry!

14 **Complete with the present perfect or the past simple.**

1 **A**: ......*Has*...... Emma ....*given*...... you her email address?

B: She ..*sent*.......... me an email yesterday, so I've got it.

2 **A**: .... you .... this musical? (see)

B: Yes, it's great! I .... it when I was in London last month. (see)

3 **A**: .... your parents .... your office? (visit)

B: Yes, they .... last week. (come)

4 **A**: .... you .... anything to drink? (have)

B: I .... some tea and a glass of orange juice at breakfast. (have)

15 **Read and complete with the present perfect or the past simple.**

TeenLink

The Unwanted Painting

by Harry Davis

The painting in the photo [1] .*has been*..... (be) in Mr Tanner's family for years. His grandfather [2] .... (buy) it for £5 in a junk shop forty-five years ago. However, he wasn't sure he liked it, so he [3] .... (store) it in his attic and [4] .... (forget) all about it until 1990. Then he [5] .... (decide) it to give it to his grand-daughter as a wedding present. The new bride hated the painting, so she [6] .... (give) it to her brother, Mick Tanner, who [7] .... (be) the owner of the painting ever since. 'I can't say I know anything about art,' says Mr Tanner 'but I [8] .... (always / like) this painting; that's why I [9] .... (put) it up in the café I own in Hillview Road. To be honest, I [10] .... (never / think) it was worth anything much.'

Imagine Mr Tanner's surprise when, a few weeks ago, a new customer [11] .... (inform) him that the painting might be worth around £500,000. The customer, a well-known art dealer, [12] .... (recognise) the signature on the painting the minute he saw it. It was by Renoir, one of the most famous artists of the 19th century!

16 **Read the information.**

Present perfect continuous	Time markers	
We use the present perfect to talk about	*for*	*They've been singing for two hours.*
• something that started in the past and is still happening now.	*since*	*It's been raining since 6 o'clock.*
I've been working on this project since January.	*all day /*	*You've been talking on the phone all morning!*
Sam's been sleeping for ten hours.	*morning /*	
• an activity that has recently stopped but it influences the present in some way.	*afternoon / evening*	
	lately /	*They haven't been doing well at school lately.*
You've got paint on your clothes. (dirty clothes = present influence of the activity)	*recently*	
I've been working on my art project. (activity)	*How long ...?*	*How long has she been waiting here?*

17 **Write sentences in the present perfect continuous.**

1 I / wear / jeans / all day   *I've been wearing jeans all day.* ....
2 We / revise / for the exam / lately   ....
3 Ken / work / on this jigsaw puzzle / for a week   ....
4 They / not practice / at all / recently   ....
5 Jenny / play / computer games / since 8 o'clock   ....
6 You / read / that magazine / all afternoon   ....

18 **Ask and answer.**

1 A: *Have you been sitting here* .... all day? (you / sit here)   B: No, *I haven't* ....
2 A: .... well, lately? (she / look)   B: Yes, ...
3 A: .... all afternoon? (you / watch TV)   B: No, ...
4 A: .... this trip for a long time? (they / plan)   B: Yes, ...
5 A: .... my toothpaste? (you / use)   B: No, ...
6 A: .... on his new book lately? (he / work)   B: Yes, ...

19 **Choose and complete with the present perfect continuous.**

run   exercise   use   paint   ~~cook~~   rain

1 A: Wow! There's a lot of food for the party!
  B: Well, Mum and I *have been cooking* .... all day!
2 A: I'm going to Sam's on my motorbike.
  B: Be careful. It .... and the streets are wet.
3 A: I can't find my calculator.
  B: Ask Tricia. She .... it.
4 A: Your house smells of wet paint.
  B: Of course it does. We .... the living room.
5 A: You and your brother look exhausted.
  B: We .... all day. We're training for a marathon, you see.
6 A: William looks very fit and healthy lately.
  B: He .... regularly.

3

20 **Present perfect simple or present perfect continuous?**

- We use the present perfect continuous to put emphasis on how long an activity has been going on.
Harry has been selling homemade cakes at the school fete all morning.
  (= the emphasis is on how long he has been doing this activity)
- We use the present perfect simple to put emphasis on the result of the activity, or what we have achieved through it.

Harry has sold eighteen cakes so far.
  (= the emphasis is on the result of the activity; that is, how many cakes he has sold)
- Sometimes we can use either tense without changing the meaning of the sentence.
I have lived here for three years.
I have been living here for three years.
- State verbs do not have a continuous form.
She has known Martha for two years. ✓
She's been knowing Martha for two years. ✗

21 **Complete with the present perfect simple or the present perfect continuous.**

1 **A**: How long ......*have*...... you ......*been playing*...... (play) this game?

  B: Half an hour, and I ......*have*...... already ......*gone up*...... (go up) four levels!

2 **A**: My friend, Nastasia, ... (appear) in three films so far.

  B: I'm happy for her. I .... always .... (think) she was a very talented actress.

3 **A**: We .... (walk) in circles for the last half hour! What's the name of the restaurant? We could ask someone where it is.

  B: I don't know. I .... (forget) it!

4 **A**: Mark .... (try) to call you all day, but your mobile .... (be) busy.

  B: That's strange. I .... (not use) my mobile at all today.

5 **A**: Julia and Daisy .... (pick) strawberries for two hours now.

  B: Really? They .... only .... (fill) one small basket!

22 **Read and complete. Use the present perfect simple or the present perfect continuous.**

TeenLink

The Work Files
The Game Master by Harry Davis

This week, let's meet Ian Brody. Ian has a dream job: he's a video game developer.

TeenLink: Ian, How long [1] ..*have you been doing*.......... (you / do) this job?

Ian: I [2] .... (work) in this area for six years now.

TeenLink: Is it something [3] .... (always / want) to do?

Ian: Absolutely. I feel I'm a very lucky guy. I just get paid to do what I [4] .... (love) all my life.

TeenLink: How many games [5]........................... (you / develop) so far?

Ian: It's not a one-man job, you know. There are teams of people doing different things. Well, my team and I [6] .... (work) on our last project for eighteen months now. It's nearly ready.

TeenLink: [7] .... (you / ever produce) a game that was a big success?

Ian: Of course we have. It's called 'The Big Chase'.

TeenLink: Great! I [8]........................... (play) that game for three months now, but I'm stuck on level 11. Have you got any tips?

Ian: Sure – but only if you promise to keep them a secret...

23 **Complete with only *one* word.**

TeenLink

A Record Baker
by Beth Banks

86-year-old Mary Bakewell has [1] *lived* in her native village all her life – literally! She has [2] .... travelled further than the neighbouring town and that's a distance of only eight miles! 'I [3] .... never wanted to go anywhere else,' Mary says. 'All my friends and my whole family have always [4] .... here. I've [5] .... my husband all my life; we played together when we were children and we [6] .... to the same school. We got married when we were eighteen years old. We've been really busy [7] .... we opened our shop! We haven't [8] .... much time for travelling, you know.' Mary and her husband, Jim, have [9] .... running the village bakery [10] .... sixty-five years. Mary doesn't even want to hear about retiring. 'The people of this village have been [11] .... our bread and cakes for ages and I have not had any complaints so [12] ....! Anyway, in the shop, Jim and I see and talk to so many people every day. It will be very boring if we stop!'

24 **Answer about you.**

1 Have you ever been abroad? Where did you go? When?
   ....
   ....

2 What changes have there been in your town in the last twenty years?
   ....
   ....

3 Have you been doing anything different lately?
   ....
   ....

Writing practice

25 **Be a reporter for *TeenLink*.**

Write an article (60–80 words) about a famous person you admire. Write about:

• how long you have known about him / her
• what he / she has done so far
• how he / she started his / her career
• what he / she has been doing recently

....
....
....
....
....

The future

'*Will*', '*going to*', present continuous, present simple, future continuous, future perfect

1. **Lucy, why are you dressed like that?**

   I'm playing a fortune teller in the school play next week. Come on, I'll tell you your fortune.

2. In ten years' time you'll be managing your own company. You'll be making the best toys and games in the world! You'll be rich and famous! In twenty years you'll have conquered the world!

   Great! Can you see the nearer future, too?

   Really? When?

   Oh, yes! You're a kind young man, Peter Hardy. And very generous, too. You are going to give money to someone very soon.

   Now. Christina and I are going to the cinema tonight and I'm broke. Will you lend me ten pounds?

3. Of course I will. In ten years' time!

   Oh, how funny! Ha! Ha!

---

1 **Complete the tables.**

Will	
Positive	He will be a famous businessman. They .... come tomorrow.
Negative	He will not (won't) be a famous businessman. They will not (.................) come tomorrow.
Question	Will he .... a famous businessman? .... they come tomorrow?

Going to	
Positive	She is ('s) going .... write a note. We .... ('re) going to see him later.
Negative	She .... not (isn't) going to write a note. We are not (.................) going to write a note.
Question	.... she going to write a note? Are we .... to see him later?

24

Present continuous	
Positive	She .... ('s) taking part in a play next week.
Negative	She is not (isn't) .... part in a play next week.
Question	.... she taking part in a play next week?

Present simple	
Positive	Our train leaves at 9.30. The doors open at 8.00.
Negative	Our train does not (doesn't) leave at 9.30. The doors do not (don't) open at 8.00.
Question	Does our train leave at 9.30? Do the doors open at 8.00?

2 **Read the information.**

Will

We use *will*

- to say what we think, guess or know will happen in the future. We often use it with *I think, I hope* or *I'm sure.*

I think they'll agree to our plan.

In 2100, people will use flying vehicles instead of cars.

- when we decide to do something on the spot.

We haven't got any juice. I'll go to the corner shop and get some.

- to promise to do something.

Don't worry, I'll fix your bike tomorrow.

- to offer to help somebody.

I'll help you with the washing up, Mum.

- to make a request.

Will you do me a favour, please?

Be going to

We use *be going to*

- to make a prediction, when something in the present already shows us what is going to happen in the future.

Look! The skier has lost his balance. He's going to fall!

- to talk about what we intend to do in the future.

We're going to take part in a TV quiz.

Present continuous

We use the present continuous

- to talk about definite plans and arrangements in the future.

She's leaving tomorrow.

Present simple

We use the present simple

- to talk about timetables and scheduled events (= events that have been officially programmed for a specific time in the future).

The concert begins at 8.30.

The next bus goes to the town centre.

Time expressions

today, tonight, tomorrow

one day, sometime in the future, when he grows up

next Thursday / weekend / week / month / year

this week / weekend / month / year

in June / the summer / 2030 on Monday

3 **Choose and complete with *will* + verb.**

show   finish   play   be   ~~climb~~   not leave   lend   not be

1 One day I .....'ll climb...... Mount Everest.
2 .... you .... very careful with my MP3 player?
3 I'm bored. I think .... a computer game.
4 They .... the project next week, I promise.
5 Mum, ... you .... me how to make a cake?
6 She's promised she .... late for school tomorrow.
7 I haven't got an umbrella with me. George, ... you .... me yours?
8 Don't worry, I .... the house without you.

4 Write sentences with *going to*.

1 *She's going to be very angry* .... when she sees this mess. (she / be / very angry)
2 ....? (you / miss / your old school)
3 .... You can take it. (I / not need / the car today)
4 .... (Daniel / not come / to the cinema with us)
5 ....? The computer won't print my work! (What / I do)
6 .... from now on. (we / start / exercising more)

5 Choose and write.

A	a promise	D	~~an on-the-spot decision~~
B	I think this will happen	E	an offer
C	intention to do something	F	a prediction based on what I see

1 **A**: Granny's said she's not feeling very well.
   B: Oh, dear. I'll visit her straight after work then. `D`
2 In the future, people won't need reading glasses. We'll all have laser eye surgery. ☐
3 You're playing badly, today. I think you're going to lose this game. ☐
4 I know you don't believe me, but I'll work really hard this time. ☐
5 I'm going to finish this book today even if I have to stay up all night! ☐
6 **A**: I can't lift this armchair. It's too heavy.
   B: It's all right, Kate. I'll help you carry it. ☐

6 Complete with *will* or *going to*.

1 **A**: I'm afraid the only free room we have is rather small.
   B: It's OK. I'm sure my brother *won't mind* .... (mind).
2 Look at all those clouds! It .... (start) raining any minute now.
3 **A**: I can't let you take my camera on the school trip.
   B: Oh, please, Mum! I .... (be) very careful with it!
4 **A**: I've got a terrible headache.
   B: Lie down on the sofa and I .... (get) you some paracetamol.
5 **A**: Your sister is an excellent dancer.
   B: Yes, she is. She .... (study) at the Royal Academy of Dance.
6 **A**: My brother's got a new job in London.
   B: .... he .... (move) there?
7 **A**: .... you .... (lend) me your book? I've left mine at school.
   B: Yes, of course. Here you are.
8 **A**: It's my birthday next Saturday.
   B: .... you .... (have) a party?

7 Circle the correct answer.

1 The film (starts) / is starting at 6 o'clock.
   Don't be late.
2 They have / 're having a barbecue next Saturday.
3 We go / 're staying at home tonight.
   We've been out a lot lately.
4 The concert lasts / is lasting two hours.

5 The holidays start / are starting earlier this year.
6 I cook / 'm cooking dinner tonight.
   Would you like to come?
7 His plane arrives / is arriving early in the morning.
8 They go / 're going on holiday in September.

8 Complete with *will* or the present continuous.

Beth: I [1] .....'m going..... (go) to the shops this afternoon.

Peter: I [2] .... (come) with you.

Beth: But you [3] .... (help) Harry with *TeenLink* this afternoon.

Peter: That's right. [4] We .... (do) the printing.
[5] .... you .... (do) me a favour, then? I need some blank CDs.

Beth: I [6] .... (get) you some from the music shop.

Peter: Thanks. [7] .... you .... (take) the bus?

Beth: No, my dad [8] .... (drive) me. He's got some shopping to do, too.

Peter: I [9] .... (bring) you some money.

Beth: No, don't worry. I'm sure the CDs [10] .... (be) expensive. You can pay me later.

Peter: Thanks Beth, you're great!

9 Complete the tables.

Future continuous				
Positive	I / You / He / She / It We / You / They	will		watching TV.
Negative	I / You / He / She / It We / You / They	.... not be (won't be)		watching TV.
Question	Will		I / you / he / she / it we / you / they	be .... TV?

Future perfect				
Positive	I / You / He / She / It We / You / They	will		written a book.
Negative	I / You / He / She / It We / You / They	will .... (won't) have		written a book.
Question	....		I / you / he / she / it we / you / they	have written a book?

10 Read the information.

Future continuous

We use the future continuous
• to talk about something that will be in progress at a certain time in the future.

I'm not free at six o'clock tomorrow. I'll be watching the match on TV.

We'll be lying on a beach this time next week.

Time expressions

at (11 o'clock)/ on (Monday morning)

this time next Monday / week / month / year

in (two days) / in (six years') time

when (you come back)

Future perfect

We use the future perfect
• to talk about something that will have finished before a certain time in the future.

I'll have done all my homework before 5 o'clock.

They will have left home by the time you get there.

Time expressions

by (10 o'clock) / by then / by the time (he arrives)

before / after (we leave) / (6.30) / tomorrow / tomorrow (morning) / (Tuesday) etc

4

11 **Choose and complete with the future continuous.**

edit *TeenLink*   ~~eat a sandwich~~   sleep on the sofa   paint the shed   have a cup of tea   read a novel

What will they be doing at 4 o'clock tomorrow afternoon?

1    2

1 *Peter will be eating a sandwich.*

2 Lucy ....
....

3 Mr and Mrs Hardy ....
....
....

3    4

4 Mr Davis ....
....

5 Harry ....
....

6 Cosmo and Bella ....
....

5    6

12 **Write sentences in the future continuous.**

1 we / fly / to Paris
   We'll be flying to Paris .... this time tomorrow.

2 you / work / in London
   .... in five years' time?

3 I / not / do anything
   .... at 12 o'clock. I'll be free.

4 Dan / have a music lesson
   .... tomorrow afternoon.

5 She / not study
   .... at 12 o'clock at night! It's too late.

6 Dad / wait / for us at the airport
   .... when we arrive?

7 We / not play / football
   .... with the boys on Saturday morning.

13 **Choose and complete with the future perfect.**

not pay   realise   finish   leave   ~~change~~   save   grow   sell

Christina: What do you think life will be like when you're eighteen?

Lucy: I ¹ _will have changed_ .... the colour of my hair, that's for sure! People won't call me 'carrot top' any more! I ² .... at least 10 cm taller and I ³ .... school. Hurray!

Christina: ⁴ .... Peter .... home to go to college?

Lucy: You bet! I'll move into his room – it's bigger. I'm sure he ⁵ .... back any of the money he owes me, though!

Christina: ⁶ .... you .... any paintings?

Lucy: Yes, to Mum and Dad!

Christina: I think I ⁷ .... enough money to go on a trip round Europe. Would you like to come with me?

Lucy: I'd love to. By then my parents ⁸ .... I am old enough to go on holiday alone!

14 **Read the information.**

> **When, as soon as, by the time, before, after**
> We do not use the simple future or future perfect after *when, as soon as, by the time, before* and *after*.
> When we finish our work, we'll go to the park. ✓
> ~~When we'll finish our work, we'll go to the park.~~ ✗
>
> They'll call us as soon as they have some news. ✓
> ~~They'll call us as soon as they'll have some news.~~ ✗
>
> I will have left before you get up tomorrow. ✓
> ~~I will have left before you'll get up tomorrow.~~ ✗
>
> We'll talk about the book after you have read it. ✓
> ~~We'll talk about the book after you will have read it~~ ✗

15 **Circle the correct answer.**

1 Don't forget to close the windows before you (leave) / 'll leave.
2 They're / 'll be pleased when you tell them the news tomorrow.
3 I'll take the rubbish out before I 'll go / go to bed.
4 By the time she will come / comes back, everything will be ready.
5 She'll travel round the world after she 'll have finished / 's finished her studies.
6 When you'll read / read the book you'll understand what I mean.
7 Come and see me after you 've finished / will have finished.
8 We'll have painted / 've painted the whole house by the time they come back from their holiday.

4

16 **Complete with the present simple or *will*.**

1 I'll finish this exercise before we ...*have*........ (have) dinner.

2 .... you .... (look) after my cats when I go on holiday next month?

3 She won't buy the new computer before I .... (see) it.

4 They .... (call) us on our mobile as soon as they arrive.

5 By the time he .... (return) I'll have fixed the broken door.

6 As soon as it .... (start) to rain we'll carry everything inside.

7 She .... (buy) a car after she has learned how to drive.

8 He'll change his clothes when he .... (get) back to the hotel.

9 After you have washed the dishes, ... you .... (dry) them, too?

10 He'll get the new version of this game as soon as it .... (come) out.

17 **Circle the correct answer.**

1 This time tomorrow I'll travel /(I'll be travelling) to Paris.

2 We'll have packed our bags / be packing by 3 o'clock.

3 As soon as you will be seeing / see him, tell him to call his parents.

4 Will you help / Do you help me with my English homework next time?

5 He will be singing / 's going to sing. Look, he's brought his guitar.

6 The train is leaving / leaves at 4 o'clock. Don't be late.

7 Do you do / Are you doing anything special this weekend?

8 I think she'll like / will be liking your present.

9 Is he really going to eat / Will he really be eating all those biscuits?

10 We will have left / will leave before you arrive, so here are the keys to the flat.

18 **Read and complete. Use *will*, the future continuous, future perfect or present simple.**

TeenLink

A Look Into the Future

by Danny McKee

Air pollution is a big problem, so I think we [1] .... (have to) find new sources of energy. In ten or twenty years, we [2] .... (drive) biofuel or solar powered cars.

By the end of this decade, mobile phones [3] .... (change) a lot. I think they [4] .... (become) much smaller and instead of a screen they [5] .... (have) a holographic projection. When we [6] .... (make) a call, we [7] .... (be able) to see a hologram of the other person standing in front of us!

[8] .... (I / spend) a holiday in space by the time I'm thirty? I certainly hope so! Many scientists believe that in the future, people [9] .... (be able) to spend their holidays in special hotels on the moon. It [10] .... (be) the trendiest place for young married couples to spend their honey ... moon!

19 **Complete with only *one* word.**

What are your plans for the future? What will you and your friends be doing in ten years' time?

Harry Davis Year 7

Let's start with myself. I [1] *will* .... definitely go to college because I want to be a journalist. By the time I'm thirty I'll [2] .... started my own magazine – as you see, I'm very ambitious.

It's easy to say what Lucy will [3] .... doing ten years from now: she [4] .... still be painting. She's very talented, so she's [5] .... to be very successful. I also hope that she will [6] .... decided to quit playing the violin by then, as a favour to the whole world!

Beth is a brilliant photographer and interviewer. I think she [7] .... be very good on TV! She can already speak French. She [8] .... starting Spanish lessons next month – so that [9] .... be a great help. Actually, [10] .... the time she finishes school she says she [11] .... have started to learn Mandarin, too.

I've no idea what Peter will [12] .... doing in ten years' time. Maybe he will [13] .... started his own business. Then he [14] .... be able to go to work as late as he likes!

20 **Answer about you.**

1 What are you doing tomorrow?

....
....

2 How are you going to celebrate your next birthday?

....
....

3 What do you think you will be doing in five years' time?

....
....

4 What do you think you will have done by the time you're thirty?

....
....

Writing practice

21 **Write an article for *TeenLink* about the year 2100.**

What do you imagine life will be like? Write between 80–100 words about:

• life at home   • transport   • communications   • entertainment

....
....
....
....
....
....
....
....

Past tenses (2)

Past perfect simple, past perfect continuous

Chatsbridge village green.

TeenLink

It's Lonely at the Top ...

Mike Benson, the film director talks about the making of his latest film.

'We were in the village of Chatsbridge, I think. We had been filming a war scene on the village green since early in the morning, so by 7 p.m. everyone was exhausted. After the film crew had left, the village green was almost empty, except for me and my assistant – we had stayed behind because he wanted to show me something. Suddenly, I heard a voice from above. I looked up and saw a man in full paratrooper gear, hanging from the highest branches of the tallest tree. During the filming of a scene, he had jumped off a plane with his parachute, but it hadn't opened at the right time so he had landed on the tree, right in the middle of the village. The poor man had been stuck there for six hours before anyone noticed him! When he finally got down he said: 'There was a lot of noise during the filming, so nobody heard me calling for help. But I'm not complaining. I had an excellent view from up there!'

Mike Benson's new film, *'Lt Smith's War'*, is out this week.

1 **Complete the tables.**

Past perfect simple

Positive	I / You / He / She / It We / You / They	had	arrived early. left by 8 p.m.
Negative	I / You / He / She / We / You / They	.... not (hadn't)	arrived early. left by 8 p.m.
Question	Had	I / you / he / she / it we / you / they	.... early? left by 8 p.m.?

Past perfect continuous

Positive	I / You / He / She / It We / You / They	.... been	looking for a pen.
Negative	I / You / He / She / It We / You / They	had not been (................. been)	looking for a pen.
Question	....	I / you / he / she / it we / you / they	been looking for a pen?

2 **Read the information.**

Past perfect simple	Time expressions	
We use the past perfect	*by*	*By 11 a.m. they had drank four cups of tea each.*
• to talk about something that had already happened before a certain time in the past.		
Everyone had gone to bed by 11 p.m.	*already*	*Sandra had already done the shopping when I called her.*
By early afternoon I had finished the book.	*after*	*Ian phoned after you had left.*
• to talk about something that had already happened before something else happened in the past. We use the past perfect to talk about what happened first, and the simple past about what happened after it.	*before*	*We had driven twenty miles before we saw a petrol station.*
	just	*I had just finished my homework when Matt phoned.*
The train had already left (= this action happened first) *when we arrived at the station.* (= this happened after the first action)	*ever / never*	*They had never seen such a beautiful sunset in their lives.*

3 **Write sentences in the past perfect.**

1 everyone / leave By 7 o'clock .....*everyone had left*........... .
2 I / just / sit down .... when the phone rang.
3 She / not travel / by plane .... before that holiday.
4 we / invite / everyone By 30th June ....
5 He / not use / sunscreen .... on his nose and it was bright red.
6 I / speak / to Mum After .... I felt much better.
7 The doors / not open .... by 8 o'clock.
8 I / never / try .... that type of food before.

4 **Ask questions in the past perfect simple. Then answer.**

Beth had a full day yesterday. She organised her time and wrote a list.
Find out how successful she was.

1 10–11 a.m. write school essay ✓
2 11–1 p.m. finish reading my school library book ✗
3 1–2 p.m. have lunch ✓
4 2–3 p.m. wash my hair ✓
5 3–5 p.m. write article for *TeenLink* ✗
6 5–6 p.m. tidy my room ✗

1 ...*Had she written her school essay*............ by 11 o'clock? ...*Yes, she had.*...
2 .... by 1 o'clock? ....
3 .... by 2 o'clock? ....
4 .... by 3 o'clock? ....
5 .... by 5 o'clock? ....
6 .... by 6 o'clock? ....

5 Circle the correct answer.

1 When I (went)/ had gone into the classroom the lesson already started / had already started.
2 They bought / had bought some popcorn before they paid / had paid for their tickets.
3 When I got / had got to the bus stop the bus left / had left.
4 By the time she managed / had managed to open the door, the postman already went / had already gone.
5 The time of the meeting changed / had changed but no one told / had told me, so I arrived late.
6 I didn't call / hadn't called you because I left / I'd left my mobile at home.
7 When they sat / had sat down on the sofa the film just started / had just started.
8 We bought / 'd bought her a present in New York but we forgot / had forgotten to take it with us.

6 Complete with the past perfect simple or the past simple.

Mrs Hardy: Oh, dear! Lucy, why are you so wet? What happened?
Lucy: Christina and I ¹ *had arranged* .... (arrange) to
meet at the cinema, but she ² .... (not
come)! I ³ .... (already / buy) the tickets,
so I ⁴ .... (go) in by myself. After the film
⁵ .... (start), a tall boy
⁶ .... (come) and sat in front of me. I
couldn't see anything so I moved to the seat next to me. But I ⁷ ....
(leave) my coke on it and I actually ⁸ .... (sit) down on it! Look at my
trousers! I was so embarrassed! When I ⁹ .... (go) outside, it
¹⁰ .... (just / start) to rain. I ¹¹ .... (not take) an
umbrella with me so I got wet! And that's not all. I ¹² .... (just / arrive) at
the bus stop when a red car ¹³ .... (splash) muddy water all over me!
Peter: Lucy, which cinema did you go to?
Lucy: The Plaza.
Peter: Oops! Nicola went to The Odeon. She called an hour after you ¹⁴ ....
(leave). She was really angry because she ¹⁵ .... (called) your mobile a
hundred times but there was no answer!
Lucy: My mobile was dead. The battery ¹⁶ .... (run out)! Oh no!

7 Rewrite the sentences.

1 Julia used all the eggs, so there weren't any in the fridge.   **because**
There weren't any eggs in the fridge *because Julia had used* .... them all.

2 When Fred opened the door, the postman wasn't there.   **by**
The postman had left .... the door.

3 It was the first time I had won a competition.   **never**
I had .... before.

4 Dennis stopped the car and then answered his mobile phone.   **after**
Dennis answered .... the car.

5 The film started and then Brian arrived with the pizza.   **already**
When Brian ....

6 We arrived at the party and then it started to rain.   **before**
We .... it started to rain.

7 First she had a shower and then she had dinner.   **after**
She had dinner .... a shower.

8 I forgot to buy milk. I couldn't make a milkshake.   **because**
I couldn't .... milk.

34

8   **Read the information.**

> **Past perfect continuous**
>
> We use the past perfect continuous
> - to talk about how long something had been going on before a certain time in the past or before something else happened.
>
> *It was 11 a.m. Paul had been talking on the phone since 9 a.m.*
> *I'd been studying for two hours before I had a break.*
>
> - to talk about an action that had already finished in the past but its results influenced the time after it in some way.
>
> *I saw John at lunch. His eyes were red and he looked tired.* (= the results of the action)
> *It's no wonder. He had been playing computer games all morning!* (= this happened in the morning but its results could still be seen later, at lunchtime)
>
> **Time expressions**
> *for, since, all day / morning / evening etc*

9   **Write sentences in the past perfect continuous.**

1   *We had been driving for two hours* when we ran out of petrol. We / drive / for two hours
2   It was a great party. .... Alison / plan / it / for weeks
3   .... for ten years before Pam / do / the same job
    she decided to do something different.
4   .... before they arrived. We / stand / outside their house / for an hour
5   Brian had an impressive toy car collection. He / collect / them
    .... since he was a boy.
6   .... before it was ready. She / work / on that project / for weeks
7   .... since last October. They / save / for that trip
8   Driving to work was difficult as .... it / snow / all night

10   **Choose and ask questions.**

> study ~~swim~~ cook eat run water print wait

1   Their hair was wet.
    .....Had......... they ...been swimming... ?
2   The printer was out of ink.
    .... your brother .... his holiday photos?
3   I couldn't move last night. My legs hurt.
    .... you ....?
4   Maria was very tired last night.
    .... she .... for the History test?
5   He came back from school and said he wasn't hungry.
    Why? .... chocolate, again?
6   I was late and they were angry.
    .... they .... for a long time?
7   Vicky had prepared a lot of food for the dinner party.
    .... she .... all day?
8   All the plants on my balcony were dead.
    .... you .... too much?

11   **Read the information.**

> **Past perfect simple or past perfect continuous?**
> We use the past perfect continuous to put emphasis on
> - how long an activity had been going on in the past.
> - the result of an activity in the past.
>
> *She'd been watching DVDs all morning.*
> (= the emphasis is on how long she had been doing that activity)
> *By 12 p.m. she'd watched three DVDs.*
> (= the emphasis is on the result of the activity)

12 Circle the correct answer.

1 They had filmed / had been filming the same scene for three hours.
2 She knew his name because she had met / had been meeting him before.
3 It had rained / had been raining since early that morning and the garden chairs were wet.
4 The phone had rung / had been ringing six times before they answered it.
5 By the time the doors opened they had waited / had been waiting in the rain for thirty minutes.
6 By the end of the week Oliver had read / had been reading two books.
7 Before he got to level five, he'd played / been playing the game for four hours.
8 We were hungry because we hadn't eaten / hadn't been eating since breakfast.

> **Look!**
>
> Remember: state verbs do not have a continuous form.

13 Complete with the past perfect simple or the past perfect continuous.

1 When Peter got up, Mrs Hardy ...*had been baking*... for two hours. (bake)
 By 3 o'clock she ...*had baked*... six cakes for the school fete. (bake)
2 Harry and his dad .... all afternoon. (paint)
 By the end of the day they .... the garage and the kitchen. (paint)
3 We .... since 7 a.m. and we needed to have a break. (drive)
 By the time we stopped at a service area .... 140 miles. (drive)
4 I .... for a new flat for three months. (look)
 I .... at twenty flats before I found one I liked. (look)
5 The match finished at 5.30. They .... for two hours. (play)
 By the end of the season, Joseph .... in fifteen matches. (play)
6 By 10 p.m. I .... three chapters of my English book. (read)
 I .... since 7 p.m. (read)

14 Circle the correct answer.

1 We ...*had just finished*... our lesson when the bell rang.
 a had been finishing   b had just finished   c just finished
2 Mike bought the CD .... he had listened to it at a friend's house.
 a by the time   b already   c after
3 I was happy because I .... well in the last two exams.
 a had done   b had been doing   c have done
4 My friends .... to a concert before.
 a had never been   b never had been   c had ever been
5 Anna hadn't taken a map with her so she .... how to get to Tom's new house.
 a hadn't known   b had been knowing   c didn't know
6 She .... on her laptop for 45 minutes when the battery ran out.
 a had worked   b had been working   c worked
7 The runners .... warmed up and were ready for the race.
 a had already   b already had   c already
8 His T-shirt was filthy because he .... it for three days.
 a had been wearing   b wore   c had worn

15 Complete with *one* word.

TeenLink

The Lottery Ticket

A short story by Shelley Barnes

That Saturday was both the happiest and the worst day in Jack Walker's life. It was the happiest because he ¹ ...*had*......... won the lottery, and the worst because he couldn't find his lottery ticket! ² .... he and his wife had looked everywhere for it, he began to panic. Then he remembered something: on the day he had bought the lottery ticket, he had ³ .... wearing his old brown jacket. The ticket ⁴ .... in the pocket! ⁵ .... he told his wife, her face went white. The previous day, she ⁶ .... given the jacket to a charity for homeless people! Jack had ⁷ .... fainted before in his life, but as ⁸ .... as he heard this, he did!

Writing practice

16 Write sentences. Use the past simple or the past perfect simple.

¹ **Jack / not waste / any time**. ² **After / he / explain / the situation** to all his friends and relatives, they all agreed to help. By the following Saturday, ³ **they / search** everywhere; ⁴ **they / talk** to every homeless person in the town, but ⁵ **nobody / see / the jacket**.

By then, ⁶ **Jack / lose / five kilos**. ⁷ **He / not shave / for a week**. He walked the streets with red eyes, talking to himself. He looked terrible. That Sunday, eight days after ⁸ **he / win / the lottery**, Jack was out in the streets once again. He felt cold and tired so he sat on some steps to rest for a while. ⁹ **A homeless old man / come / and /sit** next to him. 'Hey mate,' he said. 'It's cold. Put that on. It'll keep you warm.' In his hands, ¹⁰ **he / have / an old brown jacket.** Jack could just see the corner of a lottery ticket in the inside pocket.

1   Jack didn't waste any time.
....
2   ....
....
3   ....
....
4   ....
....
5   ....
....
6   ....
....
7   ....
....
8   ....
....
9   ....
....
10 ....
....

17 Finish the story. (Write between 80–100 words.)

Who had given the jacket to the old man?   Did Jack tell him about the lottery ticket?
How had the old man ended up homeless?   Did Jack share his good fortune with the old man?
How long had he been living in the streets?

....
....
....
....
....

Use your English (Units 1–5)

1 **Circle the correct answer.**

Last week, Harry, Peter, Beth and Lucy [1] (went) / had been to the London Eye. When they [2] had arrived / arrived, the queue was huge. The people at the front [3] waited / had been waiting for more than an hour! Luckily though, they [4] didn't have / weren't having to wait more than ten minutes, because Harry [5] had already bought / had been buying the tickets on the Internet.

The view from the top was wonderful. Beth was particularly excited because when she was little she [6] used to be / was being scared of high places, but not any more. Lucy [7] had brought / was bringing her camera with her – she [8] wanted / was wanting to take hundreds of photos. Unfortunately, while she [9] took / was taking a photo of Peter and Harry, the camera [10] slipped / used to slip from her hands and [11] fell / had fallen onto the floor. From then on it [12] didn't work / wasn't working properly. She wasn't too sad, though, because she [13] had already taken / used to take lots of beautiful photos and her camera was quite old. She [14] 'd been asking / was asking her dad for a new one for ages!

2 **Read the information and complete the sentences. Use the present perfect simple or the present perfect continuous.**

1 He moved to London ten years ago. He still lives there.
   He *has lived* in London *for* ten years.
2 They sat in front of the TV at 1 p.m. They are still watching it.
   They *'ve been watching* TV *since* 1 p.m.
3 I turned on my MP3 player an hour ago. I'm still listening to music.
   I .... to music .... one hour.
4 Sandra started making biscuits at 4 p.m. There are forty biscuits on the table now.
   Sandra .... forty biscuits .... 4 o'clock.
5 You invited everyone except me.
   You .... n't .... me.
6 We sat here at 6.30 p.m. We're still sitting here.
   We .... here .... 6.30 p.m.
7 Peter has never seen a snake before.
   It's the first time Peter .... a snake.
8 I know Richard. I met him three years ago.
   I .... Richard .... three years.

3 **Circle the correct answer.**

1 This time next week we're going to fly / ('ll be flying) to Sydney.
2 Gina is going to take / will be taking part in a dancing competition.
3 I promise I won't / am not going to go anywhere without you.
4 They'll have / 're having lunch together tomorrow.
5 Don't worry, I will have finished / finish my homework before 4 p.m.
6 A taxi will be / is waiting for them outside their house at 6 a.m. tomorrow.
7 Are you lending / Will you lend me your dictionary, please?
8 What time does the next train leave / is the next train leaving?
9 The sky is clear. It isn't going to rain / will have rained tonight.
10 Don't call him so early. He won't have woken / be waking up yet.

4 **Circle the correct answer.**

Mick Cocker [1] ..*had always*.. wanted to be a musician. When he was six years old he could already play the piano. He [2] .... his own songs and perform them in front of his friends and family, whether they liked it or not!

He [3] .... at a friend's birthday party with his group, 'Rude Jude', when a music producer [4] .... him. Eighteen-year-old Mick [5] .... a contract for his first album two days later. Mick [6] .... and performing his own music ever since. He [7] .... a great number of tours and [8] .... millions of CDs. Now, at the age of fifty, [9] .... of retiring?

'No way!' says Mick. 'There are a thousand things I [10] .... yet. For example, next month, I [11] .... a concert from a hot air balloon! I also hope that one day the band and I [12] .... on a space station!'

1	a have always	b had always	c always had
2	a used to write	b was used to write	c had written
3	a performed	b has performed	c was performing
4	a discovered	b was discovering	c had discovered
5	a was signed	b signed	c had signed
6	a is writing	b has been writing	c have written
7	a has done	b was doing	c has gone
8	a have sold	b sells	c has sold
9	a is he thinking	b does he think	c will he
10	a have done	b haven't done	c have been doing
11	a am going to give	b give	c giving
12	a have performed	b perform	c will perform

(option 1b "had always" is circled)

Now you can ...

✔ Talk about various aspects of the present.
We eat fresh fruit every day.
They're talking to Mr Evans at the moment.
We're only staying here for a few days.

✔ Talk about various aspects of the past.
I saw Nick last night.
They used to read comics.
I was watching TV at 5 p.m.
Tom had already left when I arrived at his house.
She had been playing the piano for two hours when her mum asked her to stop.

✔ Talk about past actions and how they relate to the present.
She's locked the door. I can't open it!

✔ Put emphasis on the fact that something has happened without mentioning when.
I have watered the plants.

✔ Talk about experiences.
He has flown a plane.

✔ Talk about something that started in the past and is still going on.
She's been studying English for four years.

✔ Talk about past actions whose results we can see now.
I'm tired because I haven't been sleeping well.

✔ Talk about various aspects of the future.
He'll be fine in his new job.
I'll take the dog for a walk!
Will you help me, please?
She's going to win this game.
We're having a party next Saturday.
The plane leaves at 5.30 p.m.
Tomorrow at 10 a.m. I'll be travelling to Bristol.
She'll have gone to bed by the time we arrive.

6 Modals (1)

Ability, permision, requests, offers, suggestions

TeenLink

Are you a good friend?

1 Your friend has passed an important examination in French. What do you say?
  a Congratulations! Let's celebrate!
  b OK, so you can write French, but can you speak it?
  c I could speak French when I was three!

2 It's a hot day in the park and you'd like an ice cream. Your friend hasn't got any money with him. What do you say?
  a Shall I buy you an ice cream?
  b You could go home and get some money.
  c Can you hold my ice cream? I'll go get some lemonade, too. And don't eat it!

3 Your friend asks if he / she can borrow your MP3 player. He / She wants to listen to some music while you are busy. What do you say?
  a Of course you can borrow it! Here you are.
  b We could listen to some music together later.
  c Why don't you buy your own MP3 player?

4 Your friend has broken his / her leg, so he / she can't go to the party tonight. Everybody else is going. What do you say?
  a I'll stay with you. Shall I bring some snacks and a DVD?
  b I'll tell you all about the party tomorrow.
  c Could you lend me your new trainers for the party? You're not going to need them!

Answers:
Mostly a: You're a real friend!
Mostly b: Oh, dear, you are not very popular, are you?
Mostly c: Do you enjoy being so nasty?

---

1 **Complete the tables.**

Ability	Positive	Negative	Question
can	She can ride a bike.	She cannot (...............) ride a bike.	Can she .... a bike?
could	He .... write when he was four.	He (...............) couldn't write when he was four.	.... he write when he was four?
be able to: present	I was able to climb over the fence.	I .... able to climb over the fence.	Was I able .... climb over the fence?
be able to: past	We .... able to find the key.	We were .... (weren't) able to find the key.	.... we able to find the key?
be able to: future	They'll .... able to open the box.	They will not (...............) be able to open the box.	.... they be able to open the box?
be able to: present perfect	You have been .... to talk to him.	You haven't .... able to talk to him.	.... you been able to talk to him?

40

2 **Read the information.**

Ability

Can, could

- We use *can* + verb to talk about our general ability to do something. It has only two forms: *can* in the present and *could* in the past.

She can play the piano very well.

They could run faster when they were younger.

Be able to

- We use *be able to* (+ verb) to talk about our ability to do something. *Be able to* can replace *can* in the present, future and present perfect forms.

Tom is able to buy his own clothes.

We'll be able to see real lions at the safari park.

They've always been able to help us.

Could or was / were able to?

In the past, we use *could* to talk about our general ability to do something.

- We use *was / were able to* to talk about something we managed to do in a particular case.

He could lift heavy objects because he was very strong.

In the end, I was able to lift the heavy sofa with the help of a friend.

NOT: ~~In the end, I could lift the heavy box with the help of a friend.~~

- In the negative we can use both forms(*couldn't, wasn't, weren't able to*) to talk about something we managed to do.

They couldn't get tickets for the show.

They weren't able to get tickets for the show.

3 **Complete with the correct form of *be able to*.**

1 I *will be able to see* the manager next week. (see)

2 We .... a cheap hotel room on the Internet. (usually / find)

3 .... you .... us tomorrow? (visit)

4 The DVD player was broken so we .... it. (not use)

5 They .... since they were five years old. (skate)

6 .... she .... the show last night? (watch)

7 I'm sorry I .... you last time. (help)

4 **Write sentences with *could* or *couldn't*.**

Peter	Harry	Lucy	Beth
ride a bike (3)	skate (6)	draw (3)	read (4)
play basketball (8)	use a computer (5)	swim (6)	write (5)

1 When Peter was four years old *he could ride a bike* , but *he couldn't play basketball* .

2 When Harry was five years old .... , but................................ .

3 When Lucy was three years old .... , but................................ .

4 When Beth was four years old .... , but................................ .

5 **Complete with *could* or *was / were able to*.**

1 *Were you able to finish* the test before the bell rang? (you / finish)

2 .... Spanish well when I was younger. (I / speak)

3 .... a computer two years ago? (he / use)

4 .... the question although it was a difficult one. (they / answer)

5 It was awfully hot last night. .... at all? (you / sleep)

6 .... the Eiffel Tower from my bedroom window when I lived in Paris. (I / see)

7 He didn't have a key, but .... into the house through the open window. (he / get)

41

6 Complete the table.

Permission	Positive	Negative	Question
can / could	I can use my mobile.	I can't use my mobile.	Can / .... I use my mobile?
may	You .... play outside.	You may not play outside.	May I play outside?
be allowed to	We .... allowed to wear shorts.	We .... not allowed to wear shorts.	Are we .... to wear shorts?

7 Read the information.

Permission

Can, could

- We use *can* to give someone permission to do something.
- We use *can't* when we want to refuse permission.

You can watch TV after you have finished your homework.
They can't leave before the lesson finishes.

- We use *can* and *could* to ask for permission to do something.
- Normally, we use *can* with people we know well, e.g. friends and family.
- We use *could* when we want to be more polite, e.g. with people we do not know well or older people.

Mum, can I go to bed later, today?
Could I use your bathroom, please?

May

- We use *may* to ask, give or refuse permission.
May is more formal than can and could.
May I ask you a question, madam?
You may only park in this area if you work here.
You may not feed the animals.

Be allowed to

- We use *be allowed to* to talk about something that we have or haven't got permission to do. It usually refers to rules, e.g. school or family or work.

I am not allowed to stay out later than 9 o'clock.
Are you allowed to wear jewellery at school?

8 Ask for permission. Use *can, could* or *may*.

1 ...Can I have some cake......now, Mum?   (have / some cake)
   Yes, you *can*........................., dear.

2 ...., Mr Barnes?   (ask / you a question)
   Of course you ...., Ian.

3 ...., Sir?   (open / the window)
   No, you .... not, Tony. I'm sorry.

4 ...., Mrs Rowland?   (make / a phonecall)
   By all means.

5 ...., Miss?   (take off / my jumper)
   Yes, you ...., Angela. It is quite hot in here.

6 ...., Vicky?   (borrow / your umbrella)
   No, you .... You never bring back the things you borrow!

7 ...., Aunt Julia?   (play / a game on your computer)
   Not now, dear. I'm using it.

8 ...., Miss?   (leave / my bag here)
   Yes, you ...., Jonathan.

9 Rewrite the sentences.

1 They can't play outside between 2 and 5 p.m. (allowed)
They aren't allowed to play outside between 2 and 5 p.m.

2 Children under five are not allowed to play in this area. (can't)
....

3 We are allowed to have one short break before lunch. (can)
....

4 I can only watch TV at the weekend. (allowed)
....

5 Visitors are not allowed to use this parking area. (can't)
....

6 You can't get off a London bus while it's moving. (allowed)
....

7 We are allowed to use the swimming pool. (can)
....

8 You can't take photos of the film with a camera or mobile phone. (allowed)
....

10 Complete the table.

Requests	
can / will	Can / .... you open the door for me?
could / would	.... / Would you do me a favour, please?

11 Read the information.

Requests
- We use *can / will* to ask somebody to do something for us.
Will you make the coffee, please?

- We use *could / would* when we want to be more polite.
Could you help me with this exercise, Sir?

12 Make requests. An exclamation mark (!) means you have to be very polite.

1 Ask your dad to come to your school play.
Will you come to the school play, Dad?

2 Ask a stranger to tell you where the bookshop is. (!)
....

3 Ask your friend to come to your house.
....

4 Ask a schoolmate to lend you a pencil.
....

5 Ask the shop assistant to give you a bigger bag. (!)
....

6 Ask your teacher if you can speak to her after class. (!)
....

7 Ask your friend to lend you his camera.
....

8 Ask a neighbour to turn his music down. (!)
....

13 Complete the table.

Offers	
Shall I ...?	Shall .... bring you a cup of tea?
Can I ...?	.... I help you?
Would you like ...?	Would you .... something to drink?

14 **Read the information.**

- We use *Shall I* and *Can I* in questions to offer to do something for someone.
Shall I answer the phone for you?
Can I make your bed?
- We use *Would you like ...?* to offer something to someone.
Would you like some cake?

15 **Make offers.**

Grandma Hardy is visiting for a few days. Everyone wants to make her more comfortable.

1	Peter:	*Would you like*	an extra cushion for your back? (would)
2	Mr Hardy:	....	get you something to read? (can)
3	Mr Hardy:	Are you cold?	close the window? (shall)
4	Lucy:	....	a cup of tea? (would)
5	Peter:	These shoes don't look comfortable.	bring you your slippers? (can)
6	Mr Hardy:	....	some biscuits with your tea? (would)
7	Lucy:	Your favourite show is on.	turn on the TV? (shall)
8	Mr Hardy:	I'm going to the supermarket.	get you anything? (can)

16 **Complete the table.**

Suggestions	
Let's ...	..................'s go to the cinema.
Why don't ...?	Why .... we go to the cinema?
We could ...	We .... go to the cinema.
Shall we ...?	.... we go to the cinema?
What about ...-ing?	What .... going to the cinema?
How about ...-ing?	How about go............... to the cinema?

17 **Read the information.**

We make suggestions in many different ways.
- *Let's* and *Shall we ...?* always include the speaker in the suggestion.
- We use *Why don't (you / they, etc), (You / He etc) could ...* to make suggestions for other people to do something.

Compare the sentences:
Let's stay in and watch a DVD.
(= the speaker is included)
Why don't you both stay in and watch a DVD?
(= the speaker is not included)

18 **Make suggestions.**

1 **A**: I'm hungry.
  B: *Let's make some sandwiches.* | make some sandwiches | **let's**
  C: .... | order a pizza | **what**
2 **A**: What shall we do today?
  B: .... | go to the sports centre | **why**
  C: .... | have a picnic by the lake | **could**
3 **A**: We need to get some photos for our school project.
  B: .... | cut some out of some magazines | **shall**
  C: .... | look for them on the Internet | **how**

19 **Complete with *one* word.**

Peter is going on a school trip tomorrow.

> Lucy, I don't think this is a very good idea …

Lucy: Hi! [1] _Can_ .... I help you pack?

Peter: I don't know. I [2] .... fit all my things in one bag.

Lucy: You [3] .... put the rest in another bag.

Peter: We're only [4] .... to take one bag with us.

Lucy: What have you put in it?

Peter: I've put in my volleyball, my skates, my football boots and stuff.

Lucy: [5] .... don't you leave something out? The ball, for example?

Peter: No way!

Lucy: You [6] .... definitely not be able to fit anything else in the bag, but I've got an idea.

Peter: [7] .... you tell me this great idea of yours?

Lucy: Certainly. [8] .... you wear anything you like on the coach?

Peter: Yes, we [9] .... allowed to wear whatever we want.

Lucy: How [10] .... trying something I have in mind, then?

Writing practice

20 **A good friend has sent Mrs Hardy the email below. Choose from the prompts and complete it.**

you / water / my plants / while I'm away (request)
you / do / me / a favour (request)
you / go / with her (suggestion)

you / use / them (suggestion)
~~I / not use / the theatre tickets~~ (ability)
I / bring / you / anything from Spain (offer)

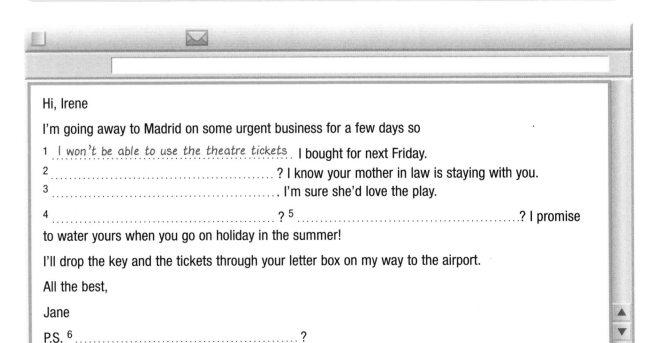

Hi, Irene

I'm going away to Madrid on some urgent business for a few days so

1 _I won't be able to use the theatre tickets_ I bought for next Friday.

2 ....? I know your mother in law is staying with you.

3 .... I'm sure she'd love the play.

4 ....? [5] ....? I promise to water yours when you go on holiday in the summer!

I'll drop the key and the tickets through your letter box on my way to the airport.

All the best,

Jane

P.S. [6] ....?

7 Modals (2)

Obligation, necessity, prohibition, advice, possibility, deduction

Mum: It might be in the wash.
Dad: No, Lucy must have taken it. I think she was wearing it when she went out.
Peter: But she's not allowed to borrow my stuff without asking!
Mum: You should remind her!

Peter: You shouldn't have taken my T-shirt without my permission!
Lucy: I know, but look: I got you this big bar of chocolate ...
Peter: All right, but you must ask next time.
Lucy: ... and your favourite comic.
Peter: Well, for this T-shirt you don't have to ask. You may borrow it whenever you like.

... and now I can go for the big stuff: his MP3 player ...

1 Complete the table.

Obligation and necessity

	Positive	Question
must **Present**	She must leave.	.... she leave?
have to **Present**	She has .... leave.	Does she .... to leave?
Past	She had to leave.	.... she have to leave?
Future	She .... have to leave.	Will she have .... leave?
Present perfect	She has .... to leave.	.... she had to leave?
need **Present**	She needs to leave.	Does she .... to leave?
Past	She needed .... leave.	.... she need to leave?
Future	She .... need to leave.	Will she need .... leave?
Present perfect	She has .... to leave.	.... she needed to leave?

2 **Read the information.**

Obligation and necessity
Must, have to (obligation)
We use *must* or *have to* in positive sentences and questions to talk about something we are obliged to do.
They must hand in their homework project on Friday.
Do all the passengers have to wear a seat belt?
- *Must* has no other tenses except the present simple. *Have to* replaces *must* in the past simple, future and present perfect.
We must get up early today.
We had to get up early yesterday.
We will have to get up early tomorrow.
We have had to get up early every day this week.

Must or have to in the present?
In the present simple, we use both *must* and *have to* with a small difference in meaning
- *must* suggests that the speaker feels the obligation to do something.
- *have to* suggests that the obligation comes from someone else.
I can't go out. I must study for the test.
(= I feel the obligation to do it)
I have to finish the project today.
(= I don't have a choice; there's a deadline)

Need (necessity)
We use *need* when we want to talk about the necessity to do something.
I need to buy a new pair of trainers.

3 **Complete the table.**

Absence of obligation	
not have to	We don't .... to go to school today.
not need to	You don't need .... answer this question.
needn't	She .... come with us.

4 **Read the information.**

Absence of obligation
We use *not have to*, *not need to* and *needn't* to talk about something we are not obliged to do.
I don't have to cook today. We're eating out.

We won't need to take our jackets. It will be quite warm tomorrow..
You needn't bring any CDs. We've got plenty of music.

5 **Complete the table.**

Restriction / Prohibition	
mustn't	You .... n't make any noise.
can't	We can .... eat or drink on the bus.
not allowed to	You aren't .... to park here.

6 **Read the information.**

Restriction / Prohibition
We use *mustn't*, *can't* and *not allowed to* to talk about something we are obliged NOT to do (prohibition), or something that someone doesn't let us do (restriction).
- *Not allowed to* replaces *mustn't* and *can't* in the past simple, future and present perfect.

- In the present tense, *not allowed to* is more formal than *mustn't* or *can't*, e.g. we use it to talk about rules etc.
You mustn't throw rubbish in the street.
They can't stay up later than 10 p.m.
We are not allowed to leave the school grounds without permission.

7 Write sentences with *have to*.

1 *Janet has to go back to work in half an hour.*   Janet / go back to work / in half an hour
2 .... when I was on the school trip.   I / phone / my parents / every evening
3 .... ? I'm trying to study.   you / make / so much noise
4 .... because his wasn't working.   Nick / borrow / his friend's CD player
5 .... before they move in?   they / paint / the new flat
6 .... three times.   Nick / rewrite / his English essay
7 .... ? Can't you stay for dinner?   you / go home / now
8 .... later. I'm too tired to read now.   I / finish / the book

8 Complete with the correct form of *must* or *have to*.

1 I *must do* .... (do) something about my hair! It looks awful!
2 I .... (go) to work an hour earlier every day next week.
3 .... (you / wear) a uniform at school?
4 My school bag is torn in two places. I .... (buy) a new one.
5 .... (Dad / watch) the news on TV now? I'm watching a DVD.
6 Our PE teacher said we .... (shower) before we went into the pool.
7 I .... (invite) David. He's a really good friend.
8 James had hurt his leg so we .... (call) the doctor.

> **Look!**
>
> Tip: we use *must* when we feel the obligation ourselves, and *have to* when the obligation comes from someone else.

9 Rewrite the sentences.

1 We must go away for the weekend more often. (need)
We need to go away for the weekend more often.

2 I need to speak to Mum about it. (must)
....

3 Must you tidy your room now? (need)
....

4 She needs to relax. (must)
....

5 Do we need to queue for tickets? (must)
....

6 I must be more careful in future. (need)
....

7 Must we answer the question now? (need)
....

8 He needs to visit his grandmother. (must)
....

10 Complete with *mustn't* or *don't / doesn't have to*.

1 You *mustn't* ...... open the present. It isn't yours!
2 Adrian .... tidy his room. I've already done it for him.
3 I .... pay cash. I can use my credit card.
4 They .... be late. No one is allowed in after the play has started.
5 We .... wear a suit in the office on Fridays.
6 We've run out of milk. I .... forget to buy some tomorrow.
7 You .... talk to your father like that! It's very rude!
8 The boys .... go to bed early today. They can stay up late.
9 Sandra .... make any mistakes this time or she could lose her job.
10 You .... call a taxi. My dad will drive you home.

> **Look!**
>
> Tip: *mustn't* = obligation NOT to do something.
> *not have to* = NO obligation to do something.

11 **Rewrite the sentences.**

Zoo rules

1 You mustn't feed the animals.
(allowed) ....

2 You are not allowed to take photos.
(mustn't) ....

3 You mustn't make loud noises.
(allowed) ....

4 You mustn't smoke anywhere in the zoo.
(allowed) ....

5 You are not allowed to sit on the safety barriers.
(mustn't) ....

6 You are not allowed to touch the animals.
(mustn't) ....

7 You mustn't cycle or skate in the zoo area.
(mustn't) ....

8 You are not allowed to disturb the animals.
(mustn't) ....

12 **Complete the tables.**

Advice / Criticism

should	Positive	Negative	Question
present / future	We should tell him.	We should .... tell him.	Should (shouldn't) we .... him?
past	We should have told him.	We should not (................) have told him.	Should / Shouldn't we .... told him?

ought to			
present / future	You ought to go.	You .... not (oughtn't) to go.	Ought you .... go?
past	You ought to to have gone.	You ought not (................) to have gone.	.... you to have gone?
had better	He'd better tell the truth.	He'd .... not tell the truth.	

13 **Read the information.**

Advice / Criticism
- We use *should, ought to* and *had better* to give advice.

You should eat more fruit and vegetables.
He shouldn't smoke.
They ought to work harder.
You'd better not go swimming yet. You've just eaten.

- We use *should have* + past participle and *ought to have* + past participle to criticise someone's past actions (i.e. to say what we think this person should or shouldn't have done in the past).

You shouldn't have borrowed my camera without asking me first.
They ought to have left earlier.

14 Write sentences.

1 you / exercise (should)
...You should exercise... three times a week.

2 we / buy the concert tickets (better)
.... today.

3 the new shop assistant / be more polite (ought)
.... the customers.

4 you / skate (shouldn't)
.... in the middle of a busy street.

5 Jake / leave the door unlocked (ought not)
.... at night.

6 We / take Dad's camera (better not)
.... without his permission.

7 I / turn off the computer (should)
.... or have you already done it?

8 we / call everyone (ought)
.... on this list?

15 Choose and give advice.

take some paracetamol and drink plenty of water
stay up late and work on it
ring them from my mobile and ask if they've got it
not go to work today

go back there right now
wear a white T-shirt over your swimsuit
talk to your teacher
not stay in the sun between 12–4 p.m.

1 **A**: I love going to the beach but I burn easily in the sun.
B: You should wear a white T-shirt over your swimsuit.
C: You'd better not stay in the sun between 12–4 p.m.

2 **A**: I think I've got the flu.
B: ....
C: ....

3 **A**: I haven't finished my school project and the deadline is tomorrow!
B: ....
C: ....

4 **A**: I think I've left my mobile at the restaurant.
B: ....
C: ....

16 Write sentences as in the example.

1 I went to Mary's house, but she was out, so I left.
...You should have called first... (call first) You ought to have waited for her. (wait for her)

2 We went for a walk, but William didn't have an umbrella so he got wet.
.... (borrow an umbrella) .... (not go out in the rain)

3 She left her bag on the table at the café and went to the toilet. When she came back it wasn't there!
.... (not leave it there) .... (ask the waiter to look after it)

4 I didn't have anything to wear because all my T-shirts were dirty.
.... (wash them) .... (wear one of your brother's T-shirts)

5 They couldn't remember my address.
.... (write it down) .... (ask me)

17   Complete the table.

Possibility / Probability		
	Present / Future	**Past**
may	He .... like it.	He may have liked it.
might	It might finish.	It might .... finished.
could	They .... see you.	They .... have seen you.

18   Read the information.

We use *may*, *might* and *could* + infinitive to talk about how possible it is for something to happen in the present or future (= possibility) or how probable something is (= probability).
- *May* expresses a stronger possibility than *might*. *Could* expresses a weaker possibility than *may* and *might*.

I'm wearing my anorak because it may rain during the match.

She's not happy in this school. She might go to another one next year.
The house is dark. They could be out.
- We use *may*, *might* or *could* + *have* + past participle to talk about possibility and probability in the past.

I may have left my keys at home.
She might have moved to London.
They could have gone to Ken's house.

19   Choose and answer the questions.

work in a bank   be on holiday   rain   go to John's house for dinner   be asleep
prefer a pair of earrings   ~~be in the garden~~   get cold in the evening

1   **A**: Where are the boys?   **B**: They .*may be in the garden* .... (may)
2   **A**: Why are you taking your jacket?   **B**: It .... (could)
3   **A**: Has she got any plans for tomorrow evening?   **B**: She .... (might)
4   **A**: I haven't seen Joe for a week. Is he away?   **B**: He .... (may)
5   **A**: Would she like perfume for her birthday?   **B**: I'm not sure. She .... (might)
6   **A**: Why don't we have a barbecue next Saturday?   **B**: The weather hasn't been very good lately.
                                    It .... on Saturday. (could)
7   **A**: What does he do for a living?   **B**: I'm not sure. He .... (might)
8   **A**: Shall I call Pam now?   **B**: No, don't. She .... (may)

20   Complete with the past participle.

1   You could .*have phoned* .... to say you were all right. (phone)
2   They might .... the car to the garage. (take)
3   He may .... this film. (see)
4   You might .... yourself. (hurt)
5   She could .... them her phone number. (give)
6   The police called. They may .... your purse. (find)

7

21 Rewrite the sentences.

1 Maybe they sent the email to the wrong address. **might**
They *might have sent the email* to the wrong address.

2 Perhaps he didn't know the answer. **may**
He .... the answer.

3 Maybe it was too late to do anything. **could**
It .... to do anything.

4 Perhaps they forgot to turn the TV off. **might**
They .... the TV off.

5 Maybe he didn't like the idea. **may**
He .... the idea.

6 Perhaps they've made a mistake. **could**
They .... a mistake.

7 Maybe she didn't see you among all those people. **might**
She .... among all those people.

8 Perhaps John took your sunglasses by mistake. **could**
John .... by mistake.

22 Answer about you.

1 What will you do after school tomorrow?
(may) *I may* ....

2 What will your parents give you for your birthday?
(might) They ....

3 You can't find your History book. What happened to it?
(may) I may have ....

4 You called your friend, but he wasn't at home.
(could) He / She ....

23 Read the table.

Deduction	Present	Past
must	They must be in the classroom.	We must have bought the wrong CD.
can't	She can't like this kind of music.	He can't have been ill.

24 Read the information.

- We use *must* and *can't* when we want to talk about something that we do not know for a fact – we are only guessing based on the information we have.
- *Must* means 'I am almost certain that this is true' and *can't* means 'I am almost certain this is not true'.
- We use *must* / *can't* + infinitive when we talk about the present.

It's very late. They must be in bed.
She can't have a cat. She's allergic to them.
- We use *must* / *can't* + *have* + past participle when we talk about the past.
He must have read the book. He bought it a few weeks ago.
It can't have rained. The streets aren't wet.

25 Complete with *must* or *can't*.

1 She *must* really like chocolate. She eats it every day.

2 They .... have been at the sports centre. I would have seen them.

3 He .... have missed the bus. That's why he was late.

4 I .... be tired. I keep making mistakes all the time.

5 It .... have been a UFO. I'm sure it was an aeroplane.

6 You .... have written the wrong phone number. This one doesn't exist.

7 They .... live very close to the school. It takes them half an hour to walk there.

8 We .... speak French very badly. No one understands us!

26 **Write.**

1 _The woman in the photo can't be Jenny_ . She doesn't look like her. The woman in the photo / be / Jenny

2 _Mr Blake must have moved_ . There's another name on the doorbell. Mr Blake / move

3 .... It is too small for me. This shirt / be / the right size

4 .... We met at George's last Tuesday. They / remember / me

5 .... All the white clothes in the wash have turned pink! You / put / something red in the washing machine by mistake.

6 .... I've just seen her outside the bookshop. Anna / be / at home

7 .... She wasn't even in the house when it happened. Eva / break / the vase

8 .... You drink six cups a day! You / like / green tea

9 .... Her husband is terrified of planes. They / fly / to New York

10 .... Was it the right one? It / be / a difficult decision

> **Look!**
>
> **Tip:** _Must / can't_ + infinitive for the present.
> _Must / can't_ + _have_ + past participle for the past.

27 **Circle the correct answer.**

Hi Lucy!

I'm having a great time with aunt Julia. We're staying in a cottage just outside the village. Aunt Julia's very relaxed about house rules: we [1] _don't have to_ make our beds, for instance. She says we [2] .... more relaxed and that we [3] .... follow rules now that we are on holiday. Isn't she great?

We visit the village every day. I've made two new friends there: Gina and Jo. You [4] .... know Gina – she's Harry's cousin. It's a small world, isn't it?

Tomorrow we [5] .... the castle near the lake – again. Well, we tried to go there yesterday, but there was a 'slight' problem. We [6] .... twenty miles or so, when, right in the middle of nowhere, the car stopped. At first we thought it [7] .... broken down, but then aunt Julia realized that the car had run out of petrol. She [8] .... have filled it up before we left, but she forgot. Anyway, we [9] .... all the way to the next petrol station and back. It took us two hours! I [10] .... check myself that the tank is full before we leave this time…

Bye for now!

Sophie

1 a needn't   b don't have to   c mustn't
2 a should be   b better   c can't
3 a need   b can't have   c don't need to
4 a need to   b must   c can't
5 a may visit   b may have visited   c 'd better visit
6 a must have driven b must drive   c ought to have driven
7 a has to have   b could   c must have
8 a should   b must   c ought
9 a had to walk   b must walk   c must have walked
10 a needn't   b 'd better   c can't

Conditionals

Zero conditional, first conditional, second conditional, third conditional

What's your jinx*?

jinx (n) a person or thing that brings bad luck

When I take an umbrella with me, it never rains. If I leave it at home, it always pours!
(Mick, 14)

I've got a pair of lucky brown trousers and I always wear them when we've got a test. If I didn't wear them, I would fail!
(Rodney, 13)

I never get what I want in shops! For example: if I order orange juice, they will only have lemonade. If I like a pair of jeans they won't have them in my size. If I ask for a ham sandwich, they'll give me a cheese sandwich. The list could go on forever ...
(Mariella, 12)

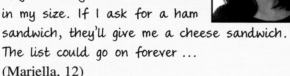

When I go out with my cousin, there's always a catastrophe. The last time we went to a restaurant, the kitchen caught fire! If he hadn't been there with us, nothing would have happened!
(Pauline, 15)

1 **Read the tables.**

Zero conditional (always)	
If / When + present → present	If you live in Australia, January is in the middle of summer.
	When you buy something, you get a receipt.

First conditional (present or future time)	
If + present → *will*	If I finish my homework early, I will ('ll) go out with my friends.
If + present → imperative	If you like this CD, take it.
If + present → modal	If she has the time, she might visit us.

Second conditional (present or future time)	
If + past → *would* + infinitive	If I had a baby sister, I would ('d) look after her.
If + *was / were* → *would* + infinitive	If I were you, I would not (wouldn't) wear these jeans.
If + past → modal + infinitive	If you told them the truth, they may not believe you.

Third conditional (past time)	
If + past perfect → *would have* + past participle	If she hadn't woken me up, I would ('d) have missed my plane.
If + past perfect → modal + *have* + past participle	If you had been more careful, you might not have had the accident.

2 **Read the information.**

Zero conditional

Form

If / When + present simple → present simple

←————————————→ ←————————————→
 If clause   main clause

- In the zero conditional we can use *when* instead of *if*.

When we go to the cinema, we eat popcorn.

- We put a comma between the *if* clause and the main clause.

If she doesn't like the food, she doesn't eat it.

- We can start the sentence with the main clause.

They walk to school when the weather is good.

Use

We use the zero conditional to talk about something that is always true, i.e. a general truth, a natural law, a scientific fact or a strong habit.

If you add salt to water, it dissolves.

When winter is near, birds fly to warmer climates.

3 **Complete.**

1 When ....*it's*.......... cold, we ....*turn*.......... the heating on. (be, turn)

2 If Nick .... the bus, he .... to school. (miss, walk)

3 .... Leo .... his computer when he .... a break? (turn off, have)

4 If I .... very busy, I .... to the gym. (be, not go)

5 .... you .... to bed early if you .... to wake up early? (go, need)

6 Ellie always .... a bottle of water with her when she .... in the park. (take, run)

7 If they .... at home, their answering machine .... a message. (not be, take)

8 If she .... a present, she .... it back to the shop and changes it. (not like, take)

4 **Choose and write zero conditional sentences.**

TeenLink

The ... Wet Quiz

| becomes ice | heat water | not drink enough water | boil water | they die | heat ice |

1 If you ...*heat water*... to 100ºC, it boils.
2 If you freeze water, it ....
3 If you ...., it melts.
4 If you ...., you feel dizzy.
5 If you water some plants every day, ...
6 If you ...., it becomes steam.

5 Read the information.

First conditional

Form

If + present simple → *will* + infinitive
If + present simple → imperative
If + present simple → modal verb + infinitive

←——————→   ←——————→
If clause   main clause

• In a negative *if* clause we can use *unless*
  (= if not) instead of *if* and the positive form of
  the verb.
If John isn't tired, we'll go out.
Unless John is tired, we'll go out.

Use

• We use the first conditional to talk about
  something that can possibly or probably
  happen in the present or future.
If they invite us to dinner, we'll go.
If you don't want this sandwich, give it to me.
If I train hard, I might win the race.

6 Write sentences in the first conditional with *will*.

1 I / have / time → I / read a magazine   If I have time, I'll read a magazine. ....
2 you / charge / the batteries → the camera / work   ....
3 it / snow → they / cancel / the game   ....
4 he / tell / the truth → he / feel better   ....
5 we / not go now → we / be late for dinner   ....
6 I / come / with you → you / buy me / lunch   ....
7 she / not pass / the exam → be / upset   ....
8 the dog / need / to go for a walk → you / take / it ....
9 the car / not start → we / take a taxi   ....
10 you / like / chocolate → you / love / these biscuits ....

7 Read, choose and complete.

| miss your train | lose his sunglasses | book in advance | hurt himself |
| turn on the air conditioning | ~~make you something to eat~~ | be better for his career |

1 If you are hungry, I could make you something to eat . (could)
2 It .... if he moved to London. (might)
3 If it's hot, I .... (can)
4 If he isn't careful, he .... (may)
5 You .... if you want a cheaper ticket. (should)
6 He .... if he doesn't put them in his pocket. (could)
7 If you don't hurry up, you .... (might)

8 Finish the sentences so they are true for you.

1 If I am late for school, ...
2 If the weather is good tomorrow, ...
3 If you don't like this film, ...
4 If we have enough money, ...
5 If you find my book, ...
6 If they go on holiday, ...

9   **Choose and complete.**

Mrs and Mrs Hardy are away for the weekend. Mrs Hardy's sister, Cath, is looking after Peter and Lucy. Complete the list Mrs Hardy has left for her.

(ask) her to call me on my mobile
(use) the cash card I've left for you
(make) sure he takes his gym bag with him
(remind) her to tidy her room
(not forget) to turn on the alarm system
~~(not feed) him~~

Dear Cath,

[1] If Harry's cat, Cosmo, comes round, ...don't feed him........ . The vet has him on a special diet because he's too fat. [2] If you go out, ... [3] If Ms Dickinson calls, ... [4] If the children need any money, please .... [5] If Lucy forgets, ... [6] If Peter goes to the swimming pool, ...

Thanks!

10   **Complete with *if* or *unless*.**

1   You can't drive a car ...*unless*........ you have a driving licence.

2   .... you don't help me, I won't be able to move the sofa.

3   Sandra won't come to the party .... you apologise to her.

4   We'll have lunch in the garden .... it rains.

5   .... there's no cheese, will you make me a ham sandwich?

6   They might leave without me .... I am late.

7   I can't write about the film .... I see it.

11   **Rewrite the sentences.**

1   If you eat sensibly, you'll be healthy. (unless) *Unless you eat sensibly, you won't be healthy.*...........

2   He might fail the exam unless he tries harder. (if) ....

3   You can't take my camera unless you promise to look after it. (if) ....

4   It won't be the same unless you come with us. (if) ....

5   If you don't know the answer, don't say anything. (unless)................................

6   Sam's parents will be worried unless he calls them. (if) ....

12   **Complete the dialogues.**

1   Peter: *What will you do if you don't pass your violin exam?*...........
        (what / you do / if / you / not pass / your violin exam)

     Lucy: .... and then I'll take the exam again!
        (If / I / not pass / the exam / I / practice / for three hours every day)

    Peter: Let's hope you pass it first time, then. .... !
        (If / you / play / the violin / for three hours every day / I / move / to aunt Cath's house)

2   Harry: .... this weekend.
        (The next issue of *TeenLink* / not be ready on time / unless / you / help me)

     Beth: Oh, dear. I have to visit my gran this weekend. ....
        (If / I / not go / she / be very upset)

    Harry: .... ?
        (you / be able to / get emails / if / you / take / your laptop)

     Beth: No, not at Granny's house. ....
        He lives next door. (I / might / be able to / get / if / my cousin / have got / a connection)

    Harry: Great! I think we can make it work.

8

13 **Read the information.**

Second conditional

Form

If + past simple → would + infinitive

If + past simple → modal verb + infinitive

If clause   main clause

- The modal verbs we mostly use in the main clause are could and might.
- When we have the verb to be in the if clause, we can use both was and were for the first and third person singular.

If he was / were a better player, he would score more goals.

Use

We use the second conditional

- to talk about what is unlikely to happen in the present, or an impossible situation.

If I won the lottery, I'd buy a new car. (unlikely)

If he didn't have bad eyesight, he would be a pilot. (impossible)

- to give advice. In this case, we usually use were when we have the verb to be in the if clause.

If I were you, I wouldn't complain.

14 **Complete.**

1 If she lived in China, she ...would speak... Chinese. (speak)

2 If there .... a late flight, would you take it? (be)

3 If they .... such a big family, it wouldn't be so crazy at their house! (find, not have)

4 If he found money in the street, he .... it. (not keep)

5 .... you .... her if you didn't have to? (invite)

6 Mum would worry if you .... (not call)

7 If I knew how to use this machine, I .... you to explain it. (not ask)

8 If they were in trouble, ... you .... them? (help)

15 **Write sentences.**

1 If / he / see / me now, he / not recognise / me. (might) ...If he saw me now, he might not recognise me....

2 I / be / happier / if / I / live / in the country. (would) ....

3 You / write / a book / if / you / wanted to. (could) ....

4 If / I / find / a taxi right now, I / be / on time. (might) ....

5 If / they / be / rich, they / travel / round the world. (would) ....

6 He / not be / so miserable / if / he / not work / so hard. (might) ....

7 If / we / take / time off work, we / go / away. (could) ....

8 If / she / not moan / so much, people / like / her better. (might) ....

16 **Give advice. Write sentences in the second conditional.**

1 **A:** My hair looks awful! (be you / go / to a different hairdresser)
   B: If I were you, I'd go to a different hairdresser.

2 **A:** It's raining hard. (be / you / not go / out)
   B: ....

3 **A:** They might not pass the exam. (be / in their place / work harder)
   B: ....

4 **A:** She can understand Spanish but she can't speak it. (be / her / go / to Spain for a month)
   B: ....

5 **A:** I'm tired. (be / you / I / go / to bed early tonight)
   B: ....

17 **Choose and write.**

TeenLink

Quiz: Would you be useful in an emergency?

1 If your friend cut her hand badly, what would you do?
   a faint
   b wrap it tight above the cut and call an ambulance
   c do nothing and call an ambulance

2 If your house caught fire, what would you do?
   a put your valuables in a bag
   b run outside and call the fire brigade
   c try to put it out

3 If someone had an electric shock, what would you do?
   a ask for help
   b turn off the electricity
   c try to pull him away

4 If a neighbour fell from a tree and hurt his back, what would you do?
   a help him to get up
   b tell him not to move and call for an ambulance
   c take him to hospital yourself

1 *If my friend cut his hand, I would* ....
2 ....
3 ....
4 ....

18 **Write sentences.**

Quiz: Would you be useful in an emergency? (continued)

Answer: The right answer in all cases is *b*.
Do you know why some of the other choices would be dangerous?

1 c   you / do / nothing – your friend / lose / a lot of blood
     If you did nothing, your friend would lose a lot of blood. ....

2 a, c you / stay / inside – the fumes / poison / you
     ....

3 c   you / touch / the victim – you / get / an electric shock / as well
     ....

4 a, c you / move / him – you / do / more damage / to his back
     ....

8

19 Write sentences.

James, Year 7   Olivia, Year 8

TeenLink

Now you can be in *TeenLink*. Add your photo and your answers to the questions.

STICK YOUR
PHOTO HERE

.................., Year 7

What would you do if ...?

1   you saw a mouse in your room?
   James: *I'd keep it as a pet.* ....   (keep it as a pet)
   Olivia: ....   (scream)
   ....: ....

2   you won £100,000 on the lottery?
   James: ....   (buy the most expensive BMX bike)
   Olivia: ....   (not spend it all – save half of it)
   ....: ....

3   went camping with your friends and they said you snored?
   James: ....   (not believe them)
   Olivia: ....   (go to see a doctor)
   ....: ....

4   you were invisible for a day?
   James: ....   (play practical jokes on people)
   Olivia: ....   (not like it)
   ....: ....

20 Read the information.

Third conditional

Form

If + past perfect → *would* + *have* + past participle

If + past perfect → modal verb + *have* + past participle

⟵――――――⟶ ⟵――――――――――――⟶
   If clause   main clause

Use

It is impossible to change something that happened in the past, but we use the third conditional

• to imagine how things might have been different.

If I hadn't been ill, I would have gone on the school trip.

They might have helped me if I had asked them.

• to express our regret about something that did or did not happen in the past, or to criticise someone's actions.

If she had been more careful, she wouldn't have broken her arm.

If the car hadn't broken down, we wouldn't have been late for the wedding.

21 **Complete.**

1 If they _hadn't left_ .... (leave) in such a hurry, they would have remembered to turn off the oven.

2 If she had read the book, she .... (not want) to watch the film.

3 .... he .... (have) a better time if he had gone on holiday with his friends?

4 If we .... (not wait) for them, they would not have known where to go.

5 .... you .... (complain) if the airline had lost your luggage?

6 If she .... (tell) me that story, I wouldn't have believed her.

7 If you hadn't had any money, ... they .... (pay) the bill?

8 If the alarm clock hadn't gone off, I .... (not wake up).

9 If anyone .... (ask) me my name, I would have told them!

10 If you .... (see) their house, you would have been amazed!

22 **Choose and complete.**

> jump on   ~~win the game~~   be able to call us   take so long   have nothing to eat
> follow the directions   not like your present   checked my essay

1 If they had played better, they _would have won the game._

2 If she .... more carefully, she would have found the right place.

3 If I hadn't brought some sandwiches, we ....

4 The train would have left without me if I .... at the last minute.

5 If he hadn't forgotten to charge his mobile, he ....

6 The project .... if we had worked on it together.

7 If he .... , he would have changed it.

8 If I .... before I gave it to the teacher, I would have been able to correct the spelling errors.

23 **Read and write sentences in the third conditional.**

1 Sophie spent all her pocket money on this T-shirt, so she didn't have any money for the weekend.
   If Sophie hadn't spent all her money on this T-shirt, she would have had some money for the weekend.

2 Mr Davis left his reading glasses at the office so he couldn't read the newspaper at home.
   ....

3 Harry went to bed at 2 a.m. last night so he felt tired all day.
   ....

4 Ms Davis had a bad cold so she didn't go to the concert.
   ....

5 Mr Hardy did too much at the gym. His legs hurt the next morning.
   ....

6 Lucy ate a huge breakfast that morning. She wasn't hungry at lunch.
   ....

7 Cosmo climbed onto the highest branch of the tree. Harry had to call the fire brigade to rescue him.
   ....

8 Peter didn't follow the instructions so he damaged the new microwave oven.
   ....

24 Choose the correct answer.

TeenLink

What's Your Best Friend Like?

My friend, Olivia, complains all the time. Last time she called me we had the following conversation:

Olivia: If my father [1] .... so old-fashioned, he would let me dye my hair green.

Me: If you dyed your hair green, you [2] .... like an alien!

Olivia: If my teacher hadn't given me so much homework, I [3] .... go out yesterday like everyone else.

Me: But, Olivia, it was a school day yesterday – no one went out!

Olivia: If my parents [4] .... me more pocket money, I wouldn't be broke.

Me: If you didn't spend all your money on clothes, you [5] .... plenty.

Olivia: If I hadn't felt ill during the last Maths test, I [6] .... the best mark in class.

Me: Olivia, you never get more than 55% when we [7] .... a Maths test.

Olivia: If you [8] .... a real friend, you'd agree with me!

Me: And if you [9] .... all the time, you would be the best friend in the world!'

1	a wasn't	b hadn't been	c isn't
2	a look	b 'd look	c would
3	a would been	b had been able to	c would have been able to
4	a gave	b give	c had given
5	a would have	b had had	c won't have
6	a had got	b would have got	c would get
7	a do	b did	c have done
8	a was	b weren't	c were
9	a don't complain	b hadn't complained	c didn't complain

25 Complete.

1 If the lesson ...was......... (be) more interesting, I would pay attention.

2 David .... (not laugh) if you told him this joke.

3 If you finish earlier, ... (call) me.

4 If it .... (not rain) we would have had dinner outside, in the garden.

5 If you're good at writing, you .... (should write) an article for *TeenLink*.

6 If I had made the reservations, I .... (book) a better hotel.

7 We .... (replace) your computer if there's something wrong with it.

8 If you .... (keep) cheese for too long, it gets really smelly.

9 If he didn't like this job, he .... (do) something else.

10 When you boil vegetables for a long time, they .... (lose) their vitamins.

11 I would have bought her a card if I .... (know) it was her birthday.

12 If I .... (have) a bigger house, I might have more pets.

26 **Choose and complete.**

there / be / a shortage of water	~~more people / recycle~~	we / turn off the tap
they / take / up to 100 years	we / stop / throwing / batteries / away	
we / protect / their environment	we / not pollute / the air we breathe	
we / not create / global warming	we / must start doing something	

TeenLink

The Environmental Issue
Here's what you say:

1 If _more people recycled_ , there
   wouldn't be some much waste. For
   example, if we dump aluminium cans,
   .... to disintegrate.

2 .... in the future if
   we don't act now. For example, if
   .... while we
   brush our teeth, we would not waste so
   much water.

3 Air pollution is the biggest problem in
   cities. If we walk more and use our cars
   less, ...

4 If we hadn't polluted the Earth,
   ....

5 If ...., many
   animal species would not have become
   extinct. If we don't want more animal
   species to die out, ...
   now.

6 Batteries thrown away together with
   normal rubbish pollute underground
   water. If ....
   together with normal rubbish we will
   reduce water pollution.

Writing practice

27 **Write.**

Complete the *TeenLink* article about the environment.

TeenLink

[We create more waste because we buy
pre-packaged meat, fruit and vegetables the
supermarket.]

If we didn't buy pre-packaged meat, fruit and
vegetables from the supermarket, we would
create less waste.

[People who work in the same area don't
share their cars, so they don't save on petrol
and they produce more air pollution.]

....
....
....

[We get information from books at school
instead of the Internet, so we waste paper.]

....
....
....

[Electrical appliances use a lot of energy. For
example, we use our washing machines at a
high temperature so we don't save energy.]

....
....
....

9 'I wish', 'If only'

Regrets, complaints, unreal present and past

1 **Complete the tables.**

I wish / If only

Present	
I wish / If only + past	.... only we knew the answer to this!
I wish / If only + *was / were*	I .... the baby was / were older!
I wish / If only + *could* + infinitive	If only I .... turn back time!

Past	
I wish / If only + past perfect	I wish they .... invited me, too.
	If .... I hadn't been so careless!

2 **Read the information.**

> **I wish / If only**
> **Form**
> * When we talk about the present we use
> *I wish / If only* + past simple
> * We also use:
> *I wish / If only* + *was / were*
> *I wish / If only* + *could* + infinitive
> *I wish / If only* + *would* +infinitive
> * With the first and third person singular we can use either *was* or *were*. We usually use *were* with unrealistic situations.
> *If only I were king for a day!*
> * When we talk about the past we use:
> *I wish / If only* + past perfect
>
> **Use**
> * We use *I wish / If only* + past simple to wish that something in the present was different from what it is right now.
> *I wish our teacher didn't give us so much homework to do!*
> *If only my parents could understand how I feel.*
> * We use *I wish / If only* + *would* +infinitive to express annoyance or to complain about something / someone else.
> *I wish you would stop making so much noise!*
> * We use *I wish / If only* + past perfect to express a regret about the past, or to wish that something was different in the past.
> *I wish she had won the first prize!*
> *If only I hadn't been so rude to him!*

3 **Match.**

1 The winters are very cold where I live.
2 I share a room with my brother and he's very untidy.
3 I enjoyed myself at the theme park, but we were only there for three hours.
4 I don't feel well.
5 I didn't go to the cinema with my friends so I was bored at home.
6 I can't drive a car because I'm too young.
7 My uncle told me how the book ended so I didn't enjoy reading it anymore.
8 I missed the school trip because I overslept.

a If only he hadn't told me!
b I wish I lived in a warmer place.
c If only I didn't have such a bad headache!
d I wish we had stayed longer!
e If only I had remembered to set the alarm clock.
f If only he would tidy up a bit.
g I wish I had gone with them!
h I wish I were older!

4 **Write sentences with *I wish / If only*.**

1 I can't invite all my friends because I haven't got a big house.
   I wish I could invite all my friends.
   If only I had a big house!

2 He can't send emails because he doesn't know how to use a computer.
   I .... emails.
   If .... a computer!

3 My dad wakes me up at 7 a.m. at the weekend. He gets up at 6 a.m.
   I .... at the weekend!
   If .... at 6 a.m!

4 She is very stressed because she works too hard.
   I .... so stressed.
   If .... so hard!

5 My brother snores and he keeps me awake at night!
   I .... snore.
   If .... at night!

6 I can't watch the match on TV tonight. I have to go to work.
   I .... the match tonight.
   If .... to work!

65

5 Rewrite the sentences with *I wish / If only.*

1 The shoes I bought are too small. (the right size)
   I wish I had bought the right size!

2 I didn't talk to him. He was very upset. (talked)
   If ....

3 I didn't know anyone at my new school. (someone)
   I ....

4 We didn't go to the beach because the car had broken down. (hadn't)
   If ....

5 I turned on the oven and left. The cake was burnt. (turned off)
   I ....

6 I got off at the wrong station. I had to wait for the next train. (right)
   If ....

7 My friend cut my hair. I look terrible! (professional hairdresser)
   I ....

8 I couldn't hear the instructions, so I didn't know what to do. (had)
   I ....

6 Choose and write sentences.

> I / can do / it   you / not wear / them   she / not be / ill   it / be / not so heavy
> ~~you / choose / a more interesting film~~   I / not lend / it to him   I / wash / it
> I / not be / rude to her

1 The film was boring.
   If only you had chosen a more interesting film!

2 This suitcase must weigh 100 kilos! I can't lift it!
   ....

3 I lent my brother my MP3 player and he lost it!
   ....

4 Vicky isn't speaking to me because I told her to shut up.
   ....

5 This exercise is too difficult for me.
   ....

6 You make a lot of noise when you walk around the house in those boots.
   ....

7 I have to go out now and my hair looks awful!
   ....

8 Mum's in bed with the flu.
   ....

7 Circle the correct answer.

1 I wish I didn't buy / ⟨hadn't bought⟩ this camera! It's too complicated to use.
2 If only I didn't have / hadn't had music lessons on Tuesdays. I always miss my favourite TV programme.
3 If only Emily didn't move / hadn't moved to another town. I really miss her!
4 I don't like milk. I wish I didn't have / hadn't had it very morning.
5 If only I chose / had chosen the other lottery ticket. It won £500!
6 I wish they listened / had listened to my advice. Unfortunately, they didn't.
7 I wish I could / had been able to help you, but I'm afraid I can't.
8 I wish we didn't accept / hadn't accepted the invitation. I'd rather not go.

> **Look!**
>
> *I wish / If only* + past simple for the present or future.
> *I wish / If only* + past perfect for the past.

8 **Write sentences with *I wish / If only*.**

1 You never agree with me!
I wish you would agree with me!

2 She didn't answer my emails.
....

3 He's always late!
....

4 I can't ride a bike!
....

5 I'm sorry I bought this CD!
....

6 You broke my sunglasses!
....

7 They make fun of me!
....

8 You didn't tell me about it!
....

9 **Read and circle the correct answer.**

Hi guys!

I'm having the worst holiday of my life! I wish I
1 *had never accepted* my aunt's invitation to join her.
a beautiful house by the sea, but I'm so bored! If only
the weather 2 .... so awful! If it didn't rain all the time we'd be able to go for walk on the
beach, at least! I wish I 3 .... so much money on new swimsuits. I don't think I'll have the
chance to wear them at all!

Mum's just sent me an email and she said that you're having a barbecue this Saturday. If only
I 4 .... with you! Just thinking about Harry's mum's barbecue chicken makes my mouth
water. I wish I 5 .... I'm going to have such a delicious lunch on Saturday, too.
Unfortunately, my aunt is an awful cook. She even manages to burn beans on toast!

Oh, if only I 6 .... you all here with me! At least if we were together, we would find
some way to have fun, even in a place like this!

I miss you all!

Beth

1	a never accept	b didn't accept	c had never accepted
2	a hadn't been	b isn't	c wasn't
3	a hadn't spent	b didn't spend	c would spend
4	a could be	b had been	c could have been
5	a had said	b said	c could say
6	a had had	b could have	c can have

Writing practice

10 **Write about you. Use *I wish* and *If only*.**

1 Write two things that you wish were different in your life now.
....
....

2 Write two regrets you have about the past.
....
....

Countable, uncountable and plural nouns

TeenLink

Health matters

'An apple a day ...'

Can you finish the sentence above? If you can, then you know all about good eating habits. If you don't, read some of the questions below. Ms Saunders, PE teacher and nutritionist answers them for you.

Q: How can I make sure I get enough vitamins?

A: Eat lots of fruit and vegetables. It's better to eat them raw because some vitamins are destroyed by cooking.

Q: Why do I have to drink a lot of water? I don't drink much water, but I drink three or four cans of fizzy drinks a day. Is that OK?

A: Nobody can survive without water. You should drink at least two litres of water a day, to help your body get rid of toxins. You may also drink some fresh juice or herbal tea, but don't drink many fizzy drinks: you'll put on weight and they're bad for your teeth, too.

Q: Is chocolate bad for you? I can't live without it!

A: Relax. There's nothing wrong with chocolate, but don't eat too much. Eat a little of everything and you'll be fine.

1 **Complete the tables.**

Some, any, no

	Positive	Negative	Question
Countable nouns	*some* He's got .... pens.	*any, no* He hasn't got .... pens. He's got no pens.	*any* Has he got .... pens?
Uncountable nouns	There's some milk.	There isn't .... milk.	Is there any milk?

Much, many, a lot of / lots of, a little, a few

	Positive	Negative	Question
Countable nouns	*a lot of / lots of, a few* He's got a .... of / .... of CDs. He's got a .... CDs.	*many* He hasn't got .... CDs.	*How many?* .... many CDs has he got? Has he got .... CDs?
Uncountable nouns	*a lot of / lots of, a little* There's .... lot of / lots .... milk. There's a .... milk.	*much* There isn't .... milk.	*How much?* How .... milk is there? Is there .... milk?

2 **Read the information.**

Countable nouns

Countable nouns are the things we can count.
These nouns always have a plural form.
One egg, three pencils, six bags, twenty people.

Uncountable nouns

Uncountable nouns are the things we cannot
count because of their nature: they do not have
a constant shape or quantity and they do not
form units by themselves. These nouns do not
have a plural form.
I need some air.
This tea smells wonderful.
Uncountable nouns are
- all liquids and gases
  e.g. *water, milk, petrol, air, helium* etc
- some solids
  e.g. *sugar, flour, butter, chocolate, sand, dust* etc
- material nouns
  e.g. *metal, wood, wool, hair, plastic, paper* etc
- abstract nouns
  e.g. *love, friendship, work, help, advice, news,*
  information, time, room etc
- generic nouns
  e.g. *furniture, luggage, money, rubbish* etc
- When we want to count quantities of
  uncountable nouns we use units of
  measurement or count their containers.
  a litre of (cream)   a glass of (water)

a bottle of (juice)   a tin of (soup)
a kilo of (sugar)   a jar of (honey)
a bar of (chocolate)   a carton of (milk)
a tub of (ice cream)   a packet of (nuts)
a cup of (tea)   a loaf of (bread)
- We use the expression *a piece of* (+ noun)
  both for concrete and abstract nouns.
  A piece of cake, a piece of metal, a piece of
  luggage, a piece of jewellery, a piece of news, a
  piece of information, a piece of advice, etc
- Some nouns appear both as countable and as
  uncountable but with a different meaning.

Plural nouns

- Some nouns appear only in plural form,
  although we talk about one unit. They refer
  to things that have two parts. We use the
  expression *(a) pair of* to count them.
  A pair of jeans / trousers / shorts / tights /
  leggings / glasses / sunglasses / scissors, etc.
  I need a new pair of jeans.
  She's got six pairs of glasses.
- Nouns that refer to a group of people or
  things are used with a plural verb.
  police, team, clothes, stairs, etc
  Our team are doing their best.
  The stairs are more tiring, but they're better
  exercise than the lift.

Uncountable	Countable
hair *Your hair is lovely.*	*a hair* *There are three hairs on the floor.*
room (as space) *There isn't any room for your clothes in my wardrobe.*	*a room* (as part of a house) *There are four rooms in this house.*
glass (as material) *Glass allows light to go through it.*	*a glass* (as container) *Can we have two glasses of water?*
paper (as material) *Paper is made from wood.*	*a paper* (as document) *My lawyer gave me three papers to sign.*
iron (as material) *Iron melts at 1,535 degrees Celsius*	*an iron* (as an electrical appliance) *If you give me an iron I'll press the clothes for you.*

Some, any, no, every

Some

We use *some* with

- countable nouns in the plural. We use *some* in positive sentences.

There are some biscuits in the jar.

I can see some people in the street.

- uncountable nouns in positive sentences.

There's some rubbish in the garden.

I've got some ice cream for you.

- We use *some* in questions both with countable and uncountable nouns when we make an offer or when we make a request.

Would you like some tea?

Can I have some strawberries, please?

- We use *someone / somebody, something, somewhere* in the same way as *some*.

Someone has left this parcel for you.

I know my keys are somewhere in the house.

Any

- We use *any* with countable and uncountable nouns in questions and negative sentences.
- We use *anyone / anybody, anything, anywhere* in the same way as *any*.

Are there any eggs in the fridge?

There isn't any water in the jug.

Is there anyone at home right now?

I don't know anything about him.

No

- We use *no* with countable and uncountable nouns in positive sentences. Because *no* is negative, the meaning of the sentence is negative. We use *no-one / nobody, nothing* and *nowhere* in the same way.

I've got no money with me.

(= I haven't got any money with me.)

There are no animals in the picture.

(= There aren't any animals in the picture.)

There's no-one in the classroom.

(= There isn't anyone in the classroom.)

There's nothing wrong with it.

(= There isn't anything wrong with it.)

Every

- We can only use *every* with countable nouns in the singular in positive and negative sentences, and in questions. We use *everyone / everybody, everything* and *everywhere* in the same way.

Every book in this bookcase is more than fifty years old.

Everyone knows this isn't true.

Is everything ready?

I haven't looked everywhere yet.

Much, many, a lot of / lots of, a little, a few

- We use these words to talk about the quantity of nouns in general terms.

Much, many

- We use *much* and *many* in questions and negative sentences.
- We use *much* with uncountable nouns and *many* with countable nouns.

Is there much water in the lake this year?

I haven't got much time, so be quick.

Have you got many emails today?

There aren't many shops in this area.

A lot of / lots of

- We use *a lot of / lots of* with both uncountable and countable nouns, usually in positive sentences. There is no difference in meaning between these two expressions.

There's lots of room for all of us here.

There are a lot of people here today.

A little, a few

- We use *a few* with countable nouns and *a little* with uncountable nouns. Both expressions have a positive meaning.

There are a few chairs here.

(= there are enough chairs)

There's a little juice in this carton.

(= it's enough)

3 **Complete with *some* or *a / an*.**

1 I've got ...*some*......... news for you.
2 Can I have .... piece of cake, please?
3 I'm not ready yet. I need .... time.
4 Can you get .... coffee at the supermarket, please?
5 There's .... open box of cereal on the table.
6 If you want .... good advice, ask your dad.
7 I'll stop on my way and put .... petrol in the car, OK?

8 Is this .... new pair of trousers?
9 There was .... traffic on the road but there were no delays.
10 I have .... idea! Let's make a card for aunt Laura.
11 She needs .... furniture for the new flat.
12 I saw .... tall man coming out of the shop.

4 **Circle the correct answer.**

1 Glass / Glasses takes 1,000,000 years to disintegrate.
2 Her hair is / are light brown.
3 There's room / a room in the box for one more cake.
4 Will you get me a / some Sunday paper from the corner shop?
5 Iron is / Irons are a very strong metal.
6 Can I have some glass / glasses of water, please?
7 Have you got an / some iron? I need to press my trousers.
8 Yuk! There's a / There are hair in my soup!
9 I'm printing my essay and I need some more paper / papers.
10 This is a / some very big room!

5 **Choose and complete.**

piece   cartons   ~~pair~~   litres   tin   loaf   bottle   pairs   pieces   bag

1 I need a new ...*pair*.......... of brown trousers. My old ones are falling apart.
2 I'll give you a .... of advice, my son.
3 I think we have a .... of bread somewhere.
4 We need two .... of juice for breakfast, tomorrow.
5 Have we got a .... of lemonade?

6 Here's a .... of sugar, madam.
7 This jug can hold two .... of liquid.
8 There are two .... of luggage behind the reception desk.
9 I want something quick for dinner. I'll open a .... of soup.
10 How many .... of sunglasses have you got?

6 **Complete with *some*, *any* or *no*.**

1 We've got ...*some*......... eggs. Shall I make an omelette?
2 There's .... furniture in the flat because we haven't moved in yet.
3 They haven't heard .... news about their friend yet.
4 Would you like .... ice cream?
5 There's .... information about train timetables. Let's ask someone who works here.

6 He hasn't got .... posters on the wall of his room. His mum doesn't allow it.
7 There are .... seats left. Shall we go somewhere else?
8 Is there .... paper in the photocopier?
9 There are .... clouds in the sky. It's perfectly clear!
10 There's .... money on the kitchen counter. It's for you.

10

7 Circle the correct answer.

1 It's beautiful here in spring. There are flowers somewhere / (everywhere).
2 I can't see the boys nowhere / anywhere. Have you seen them?
3 Is there anything / everything I can do for you?
4 I'd like something / nothing cold to drink.
5 I'll take you anywhere / somewhere nice for your birthday.
6 Anyone / Someone called you while you were out.
7 Everything / Nothing she said is a lie. She has not told you the truth about anything.
8 Betty's on the phone. She must be somewhere / nowhere noisy. I can't hear a word she's saying!
9 Everybody / Nobody knew him in the village. He was a total stranger.
10 I know something / nothing about this. Why don't you ask your dad?

8 Rewrite the sentences.

1 There's nothing in this box. (isn't)   _There isn't anything in this box._
2 I don't wear any perfume. (no)
3 I saw no-one at the station. (anyone)
4 She has no friends. (hasn't)
5 We didn't go anywhere last night. (went)
6 She never tells me anything. (nothing)
7 There are no cars on this island. (any)

9 Complete.

1 Everyone ..._knows_.. this story.   **know**
2 People .... many strange things.   **do**
3 Don't worry, everything .... all right. **be**
4 All my colleagues .... to work by tube. **go**
5 Everyone .... hard here.   **work**
6 Everything in this shop .... from China. **come**

Look!

Tip:
Everybody likes chocolate.
every(body) + singular verb

10 Complete with *much, many* or *a lot of / lots of*.

1 There aren't ..._many_.. things to do. We'll finish soon.
2 I can't fit my things into my suitcase. There isn't .... space.
3 £200 is .... money for a meal!
4 She must hurry. She hasn't got .... time.
5 There aren't .... students in my class.
6 .... people don't like eating snails.
7 Have you got .... pairs of shoes?
8 I'm afraid you haven't got .... choice. You can have the blue T-shirt or the red T-shirt.

11 Complete with *a few* or *a little*.

1 There are ..._a few_.. glasses in the cupboard.
2 Can I have .... ice cream, please?
3 I've made .... sandwiches if you're hungry.
4 There's .... orange juice in the bottle. Would you like some?
5 Could I ask you .... questions?
6 James has visited Rome. He can give you .... tips.
7 Would you like .... cream with that?
8 I finished the project with .... help from my friend.

12 **Read the information.**

Articles

The indefinite article: *a / an*

- The indefinite article *a / an* goes before countable nouns in the singular.
- We use *a* before nouns or adjectives + noun that start with a consonant, and *an* before those that start with a vowel.

a book, an orange, a big orange, an open book, a garden, an insect, a computer, an ant

- Be careful with words that begin with *eu, u* and *h*. Read them aloud first to see if their first letter sounds like a vowel or a consonant:

a house, an hour, a university, an umbrella, a European country

We use *a / an*

- when we refer to an item in general

Is there a pen? (any pen, not a particular one)

- after the verb *to be* to talk about somebody's profession, job title or ability to do something.

Sebastian is a teacher. (profession)
Zara is a very good cook. (ability)

The definite article: *the*

The definite article *the* goes before uncountable nouns, countable nouns in the singular and plural and adjectives + noun.

We use *the*

- when we talk about something specific or unique

Where's the camera?
(a specific camera, not any camera)
The moon is very bright tonight.
(unique, there's only one moon)

- before names of oceans (*the Atlantic Ocean*), seas (*the Mediterranean*), rivers (*the Nile*), mountain ranges (*the Alps*), deserts (*the Sahara desert*)
- before the names of these countries / states: *the USA (United States of America), the UK (United Kingdom), the Netherlands, the United Arab Emirates, the Bahamas, the Philippines*
- before the names of cinemas, theatres and venues (*the Odeon, the Barbican*, hotels (*the Cumberland, the Dorchester*), museums (*the Museum of National History, the V&A*), newspapers (*the Guardian, the Times*), organisations (*the United Nations*) and ships (*the Costa Atlantica*)

- before the names of families (*the Hardys, the Browns*) and nationalities (*the British, the French*)
- before collective adjectives (= adjectives we use to talk about a group of people) (*the young, the old, the poor, the educated*)
- before musical instruments (*the guitar, the piano*) and the word *radio* (*I listen to the radio*)
- before these words: *the cinema, the theatre, the bank, the post office, the station, the airport, the shops, the doctor, the dentist, the garage* etc
I've got a toothache. I need to go to the dentist.
I'd like to see this film. Let's go to the cinema.
- before: *the police, the fire brigade, the army*
- with the time expressions: *in the morning / afternoon / evening / night* but not with the expression *at night*

Zero article

Zero article means *no article* (= we do not use any article).

We do not use an article

- before proper names

Nick is in the car.

- before abstract nouns

Life in these areas can be hard.

- before plural nouns and uncountable nouns when we talk about them in general terms

Elephants have an excellent memory.
(elephants as a species, in general)
This is where the elephants live.
(this particular group of elephants)

- before the names of countries (*Italy, Belgium*), cities (*Copenhagen, Vienna*), continents (*Europe, Africa*), mountains (*Mt Everest, Mt Olympus*), lakes (*Loch Ness, Lake Titikaka*), streets or squares (*Oxford Street, Berkeley Square*) and parks (*Central Park*)
- before sports or games, school subjects and meals

Tom plays hockey.
I love Maths.

- with languages

Do you speak Dutch?
but we say: *The (Italian / Spanish etc) language*

- with the words: *home, work, school, college, university, hospital, prison, church* and *bed*

13 **Complete with** *a / an.*

1 Would you like ......*an*...... omelette for breakfast?
2 This isn't a rat, it's .... hamster!
3 This is .... uncomfortable chair.
4 What .... excellent idea!
5 How many Euros are there in .... English pound?
6 Fortunately, we do not have to wear .... uniform at school.
7 I'll be ready in .... hour.
8 There isn't .... window in this room.
9 Can you lend me .... umbrella?
10 When we go to Italy we'll stay in .... hotel.
10 Have you ever been on .... yacht?
12 I went to see .... excellent play last night.

14 **Circle the correct answer. (–) means zero article.**

1 Let me give you a / an example.
2 Do you like the / – horror films?
3 Martha is – / an architect.
4 Would you like an / – apple?
5 Is there the / – life on planet Mars?
6 I play – / the basketball for the school team.
7 She is a / the good listener.
8 Where's – / the sugar? I can't find it.
9 This is a / the house where I was born.
10 This is an / – interesting question.
11 I'd like to be a / the doctor when I grow up.
12 A / The sun sets at 6.30 p.m. today.

15 **Complete with** *the* **or (–).**

1 Have you ever been to .....*the*......... Louvre?
2 My brother's learning how to play .... piano.
3 Does your mum like .... cats?
4 I don't want to watch TV. I'm going to listen to .... radio.
5 .... French usually drink coffee with their breakfast.
6 Why don't we go to .... London for the weekend?
7 What time do you have to be at .... airport?
8 I can't speak .... German very well.
9 Is Fred at .... home?
10 Can you tell me where .... toilets are?
11 .... cheese you've bought smells funny!
12 You can't still be in .... bed! It's 11 o'clock!

16 Choose and complete.

the (x5)   a (x3)   an (x2)   any   anyone   few   some   someone   nothing   (–)

TeenLink

It was late in ¹ _the_ .... evening when Mr Clark returned home from ² .... work. As he closed ³ .... front door behind him, he heard ⁴ ....noise in ⁵ .... living room. Mr Clark did not expect ⁶ .... to be in the house, because his wife and children were away on holiday. He grabbed ⁷ .... umbrella from the hall and moved silently towards the living room. The room was in a mess! ⁸ .... had broken into the house, but whoever it was had just gone out of the open window.

Mr Clark called ⁹ .... police immediately. After they had taken fingerprints, Mr Clark realised that ¹⁰ .... was missing. The burglar hadn't taken ¹¹ .... money or valuables. On top of that, Mr Clark found ¹² .... big black bag, which he had never seen before. When the policemen opened it, they found ¹³ .... jewellery, ¹⁴ .... silver teapot and ¹⁵ .... antique clock. The policeman laughed and explained that the burglar had probably been to a ¹⁶ .... other houses before Mr Clark's and that, in his hurry to escape, he had left ¹⁷ .... stolen goods behind!

17 Complete the blanks with only one word where necessary, or a dash (–).
Then do the quiz.

TeenLink

The Whizz Quiz

Can you do this quiz in one minute? And more importantly, how many answers can you get right?

1	Supper is ....ª........... meal we eat in the morning.	True / **False**
2	Oranges have a .... of vitamin C.	True / False
3	.... French language is spoken in .... Canada.	True / False
4	.... Mississippi River is in .... Australia.	True / False
5	There aren't .... tigers in .... Africa.	True / False
6	You can listen to .... music in a library.	True / False
7	There is no water in .... Sahara desert.	True / False
8	Scotland is in .... United Kingdom.	True / False
9	A deck chair is a .... of furniture.	True / False
10	In .... Britain you dial 999 to call .... fire brigade.	True / False
11	There isn't .... life on .... moon.	True / False
12	You can see birds in .... aquarium.	True / False
13	The word 'information' is an .... noun.	True / False
14	.... New York is in .... England.	True / False
15	.... Acropolis of Athens is in Rome.	True / False
16	Venus Williams is .... famous tennis player.	True / False
17	*Titanic* sank on its second voyage.	True / False
18	.... people are allergic to peanuts.	True / False
19	They speak .... Dutch in .... Netherlands.	True / False
20	We cut down trees with a .... of scissors.	True / False

Use your English (Units 6–10)

1 **Circle the correct answer.**

1 **A:** (Were you able to) / Could you finish your work, yesterday?
   B: No, I wasn't because I must / had to go to my aunt's for dinner.

2 **A:** Ought / Shall I make you a cup of tea?
   B: Yes, please. Could you / Are you able to make me a sandwich, too?

3 **A:** I can't / may open this jar. Ought / Could you do it for me?
   B: Sure. Here you are.

4 **A:** Now, remember, children. You don't have to /mustn't touch the paintings in the gallery.
   B: How about / Are we allowed to take photos, miss?

5 **A:** Do we have / Could we use your computer, Ms Holmes?
   B: I'm sorry. I'm using it myself. You may / need to use the computer in the next office, though.

6 **A:** Do we have to / need go out? It's raining!
   B: Well, I have to / can go to the supermarket but you aren't allowed to / needn't come with me.

2 **Complete with *one* word.**

Sara: Mum, ¹ ....*can*........ you help me look for my watch?

Mrs Jones: Sure. Where did you see it last?

Sara: I was wearing it before I had a shower.

Mrs Jones: It ² .... be in the bathroom, then.

Sara: No, I think I took it off when I was in my room.

Mrs Jones: ³ .... don't you have a look in your room then? It ⁴ .... be there.

Sara: No, it isn't in my room. I've already looked there.

Mrs Jones: ⁵ ....'s have another look in the bathroom.

Sara: Oh, here it is! It was on the floor, behind the bin!

Mrs Jones: Really, Sara, you ⁶ .... be more careful about where you leave your things!

3 **Complete the conditionals.**

1 If he ...*has*........... (have) enough money, he might buy a new bike.

2 He .... (not lose) his glasses if he had been more careful.

3 She wouldn't do this job unless she really .... (like) it.

4 The machine .... (stop) when you push the red button.

5 They wouldn't have called me if you .... (not give) them my phone number.

6 If I go away for the weekend, ... (you / look) after my cat?

4 **Rewrite the sentences.**

1 If only I hadn't forgotten to lock the door!   **remembered**
   I wish ..*I had remembered to lock*.......... the door.

2 I wish I hadn't put my new jumper in the washing machine.   **washed**
   If only .... by hand!

3 If only it wasn't so hot today!   **cooler**
   I wish .... today.

4 I wish I were taller!   **so**
   If only .... short!

5 If only we hadn't gone out that day!   **stayed**
   I wish .... that day.

5 Circle the correct answer.

Hi, Harry!

Today was my first day at ¹ .....a........... new school. It wasn't too bad! I've made
² .... new friends and I've had ³ .... basketball practice (I hadn't
played basketball since I sprained my ankle a month ago). ⁴ .... the kids in
my class come from different countries, all over the world, but guess what: there are
⁵ .... other British kids in my class. I'm the only one! I sit between
⁶ .... Italian boy, called Luigi and ⁷ .... German girl, called Marta. Luigi loves football –
that's all he ever talks about!
⁸ .... of my classmates go to a karate class after school and they've asked me to join them.
I think I might go and see what it is like.

I'll write next week with more news!

Cheers, Alex

I (a a)	b an	c the	5 a no	b any	c some
2 a a few	b any	c much	6 a a	b an	c
3 a lots	b a little	c a	7 a an	b a	c
4 a Some	b Many	c A lot of	8 a Any	b Lot	c Some

Now you can ...

✔ Talk about:

ability	*I could read when I was five.*
permission	*You can leave early today.*
obligation	*We have to wear a uniform at work.*
necessity	*She needs to do the exercise again.*
absence of obligation	*They don't have to go to school.*
restriction / prohibition	*You mustn't touch this button.*
possibility / probability	*It may rain tomorrow.*

✔ Make a(n):

request	*Could you close the door, please?*
offer	*Shall I get you something to drink?*
suggestion	*Why don't we go to the cinema tonight?*
deduction	*She can't be twenty years old! She still goes to school.*

✔ Give advice. *If I were you I wouldn't buy these shoes.*

✔ Talk about something that is generally true.
If you don't get enough sleep, you feel tired in the morning.

✔ Talk about something that may happen in the present or future.
If they have time, they'll visit us.

✔ Talk about an impossible or unlikely situation.
If she knew the answer she would tell me.

✔ Imagine how things might have happened in a different way.
If you had met Leo, you would have liked him.

✔ Express regret about something in the past, or criticize someone's actions.
If they hadn't missed the bus they would have home on time.

✔ Wish that the present was different.
I wish / If only we had more time!

✔ Express a regret about the past, or wish that the past was different.
I wish / If only he had been more careful!

The passive

Present, past and future passive

TeenLink

The *TeenLink* Files: Glass

Glass is made from sand, soda ash, lime and cullet. Cullet is recycled glass that has been crushed into a powder. To make glass, the first three ingredients are carefully weighed and mixed by the glass maker. Then he / she adds cullet to the mixture. The mixture is melted in special furnaces until it looks like thick syrup. When it cools, this syrupy mass becomes glass. After it has been given its final shape, the glass is reheated and then cooled. This is done to make it stronger.

Glass can be given almost any shape. Today glass is made in factories, but in ancient times it was made by hand. No one knows exactly when or where glass was first made, but it was produced as far back as 2000 BC by the Egyptians and perhaps the Phoenicians. The oldest method used to shape glass was blowing. A ball of melted glass was placed at the end of a long iron pipe and the glass maker blew air into it, just as we do with balloons today, but more gently. This way the glass at the end of the pipe could be blown into any shape and thickness. This method is still used today to produce hand-made glass objects and objects of art.

1 **Complete the tables.**

	Active	Passive
Present simple	They make glass.	Glass is made.
Present continuous	They are making glass.	Glass is being ....
Past simple	They made glass.	Glass .... made.
Past continuous	They were making glass.	Glass was being ....
Present perfect	They have made glass.	Glass .... been made.
Past perfect	They had made glass.	Glass had .... made.
Future '*will*'	They will make glass.	Glass will be ....
Future '*going to*'	They are going to make glass.	Glass .... going to be made.
Modals		
Can	They can make glass.	Glass .... be made.
Should	They should make glass.	Glass should .... made.
Have / has to	They have to make glass.	Glass has to be ....
Infinitive	to make	to be made

2 **Read the information.**

Passive

Form

Subject + verb *to be* + past participle

Tense	*to be* → past participle
Present simple	The car is serviced → every six months.
Present continuous	Lunch is being → prepared.
Past simple	The cake was made → yesterday.
Past continuous	She was being → introduced to everyone.
Present perfect	My watch has been → mended.
Past perfect	The letter had been → sent.
Future '*will*'	The project will be → finished early.
Future '*going to*'	I am going to be → taught French.
modal + infinitive without '*to*'	This room should be → redecorated.
modal + infinitive with '*to*'	They ought to be → shown where to go.

Positive

John was introduced to Kevin.
The car has been serviced.
We were being followed by a dog.
It can be done.

Negative

John was not (wasn't) introduced to Kevin.
The car has not (hasn't) been serviced.
We were not (weren't) being followed by a dog.
It cannot (can't) be done.

Question

Was John introduced to Kevin?
Has the car been serviced?
Were we being followed by a dog?
Can it be done?

Use

• We use the passive form when we want to focus on the action itself, not who performs it. Compare the following sentences:
The hotel serves breakfast between 7–10.30 a.m.
(= active: we say who performs the action)
Breakfast is served between 7–10.30 a.m.
(= passive: the focus is on the action, not on who performs it)

• The passive form is more formal than the active form so we often use it in business situations.
You must return supermarket trolleys to their station.
Supermarket trolleys must be returned to their station.

3 **Circle the correct answer.**

1 The rooms clean / are cleaned every day.
2 I've lost / 've been lost my keys!
3 Martha is being made / is making good progress.
4 The bag was found / found in a black cab.
5 I'm being sent / sending an email.
6 German speaks / is spoken in Switzerland.
7 Your salads are prepared / are being prepared right now.
8 They might see / be seen a baby panda at the zoo.
9 This door should keep / be kept locked at all times.
10 Up to now, three new houses have been built / have built in this area.
11 His teacher has given / has been given him a lot of homework for the weekend.
12 The book will publish / will be published next spring.

4 **Write passive sentences in the tense given.**

1 *A new shopping centre will be built near the town.*

A new shopping centre / build / near the town
(future 'will')

2 ....

The car / repair / before they left (past perfect)

3 ....

The lights / switch on / at 8 p.m. (past simple)

4 ....

All the students / inform / of the changes
(present perfect)

5 ....

One of these games / sell / every minute
(present simple)

6 ....

The flowers / send / tomorrow (future 'will')

7 ....

I / take / to the Headteacher (past simple)

8 ....

The walls / paint / pale yellow (future 'going to')

5 **Complete with the passive present continuous or the passive past continuous.**

1 The class *are being shown* .... round the zoo at the moment. (show)

2 The computer crashed while the new program .... (install)

3 When Jane first saw the house it .... (redecorate)

4 Your order .... right now, sir. (send)

5 When we arrived at school, the central heating .... (repair)

6 The plane .... at the moment, so that it's ready for its next flight. (clean)

7 The show .... in front of a live audience right now. (record)

8 All the changing rooms ...., so I had to wait in a queue. (use)

6 **Write passive sentences.**

1 *Instructions must be followed carefully.*

Instructions / must / follow / carefully

2 ....

The sandwiches / could / make / the day
before

3 ....

This T-shirt / should / wash / at 30°C

4 ....

These bags / can / recycle

5 ....

The shops / might / close / tomorrow

6 ....

Your glasses / need / repair

7 ....

Young children / ought not / leave / alone at
home

8 ....

Customers / have to / inform / of the new
opening hours

7 **Complete with the correct passive form.**

1 **A**: Is the photocopier ready?
   B: No, I'm afraid it *hasn't been repaired yet* . (not repair / yet)

2 **A**: Where .... the garden chairs .... ? (keep)
   B: I usually put them in the garage in case it rains.

3 **A**: When .... this cake .... ? (make)
   B: I baked it earlier this morning.

4 **A**: There was no light in the room because the bulb .... (not / replace)
   B: I thought John had done it!

5 **A**: Someone will interview Samantha for a magazine tomorrow.
   B: Great! When .... the interview .... ? (publish)

6 **A**: The rubbish .... yesterday. (not collect)
   B: Yes, I know. All the bins are full.

8 Complete with the present simple passive, the past simple passive or the passive infinitive.

TeenLink

What? When? Who? and How?

CDs by Peter Hardy

The first CDs ¹ ...were made... (make) back in 1988 – Wow! I ² .... even .... (not born) then! CDs ³ .... (make) of polycarbonate (that's a kind of plastic). As you probably know, a CD is flexible and may ⁴ .... (bend), but only up to a point. After that it breaks, and it'd better not be your sister's! (Well, I couldn't use one of mine to test this theory, could I?) Here's a tip: old or unwanted CDs can ⁵ .... (use) as coasters!

Mini photo printer

Digital Cameras by Angela Smith

Conventional cameras used light to store images on film. The film ⁶ ...was taken... (take) to the local chemist where it ⁷ .... (process) and the the photos ⁸ .... (print) on paper. Digital cameras work in a different way. The image ⁹ .... (store) in the tiny computer inside the camera. This image ¹⁰ .... (can/see) right away through the display at the back of the camera. Images that we don't want to keep ¹¹ .... (can / erase) with the touch of a button. Finally, digital images ¹² .... (download) onto a computer or printed on a photo printer.

9 Read the information.

Agent

- The focus of the passive form is the action itself, not who does it. However, when we want to say who does the action (called the 'agent'), we use *by* and the name or noun.
- We use the agent only when by doing so we add information to our sentence or make it clearer.

The story was written by Frank Wood.
All the photos were taken by my brother.

- We do not use the agent when we do not want to give this information or when we do not know who the agent is.

All the reports have been collected.
(who collected them is not important)

Her handbag was stolen!
(we do not know who did it)

- We do not use the agent when it is easily understood or when it is vague, e.g. *someone, people, they.*

Active: *The police have arrested the thief.*
Passive: *The thief has been arrested.*
(easily understood, only the police can arrest someone.)
Active: *People do this exercise in three minutes.*
Passive: *This exercise can be done in three minutes.*
(vague, we are referring to people in general, so there is no information added by using an agent.)

Active to passive
- When a sentence is turned from the active into the passive:
- the object of the active clause becomes the subject of the passive clause (remember that only verbs that take an object can become passive verbs).
- the verb changes from the active to the passive. The tense stays the same, e.g. active present continuous becomes present continuous passive.

- The subject of the active clause becomes the agent of the passive clause if necessary.

Subject	active verb	object
Paul	has made	these posters.

Active clause

Subject	passive verb	agent
These posters	have been made	by Paul.

Passive clause

10 Add the agent where necessary. Add a cross where the agent is not used.

1 The film was directed ..*by Steven Spielberg*.. (Steven Spielberg)
2 The fire has been put out ......*X*.......... (some people)
3 *TeenLink* is edited .... (Harry)
4 A new president has been elected .... (people)
5 The Art class is taught .... (a well-known painter)
6 All the windows were cleaned .... (the window cleaners)
7 The building was designed .... (a famous architect)
8 The new sofa will be delivered .... (the delivery men)

> **Look!**
>
> **TIP:** only use the agent when it is absolutely necessary.

11 Rewrite the sentences in the passive.

1 They repaired my computer in two hours.
   My computer was repaired in two hours.

2 Tom has made the best suggestion.
   ....

3 The teacher will finish our progress reports tomorrow.
   ....

4 The taxi driver drove us to the airport.
   ....

5 The students had made posters for the school fete.
   ....

6 Someone is preparing our lunch.
   ....

7 The painter should paint the room white.
   ....

8 Someone was following me.
   ....

12 Rewrite the sentences in the passive.

1 **A:** Can they find a solution?
   B: They have already done something about it.
   A: *Can a solution be found?* ....
   B: *Something has already been done about it.*

2 **A:** Have they painted the whole house?
   B: They haven't done the garage yet.
   A: ....
   B: ....

3 **A:** Did Ashley take that photo?
   B: Yes, she did. She made the photo frame, too.
   A: ....
   B: ....

4 **A:** Did anyone lock the door from the inside?
   B: No, but somene had closed all the windows.
   A: ....
   B: No, but all ....

5 **A:** Will someone take us to the office from the airport?
   B: I don't think so. They should take us to our hotel first.
   A: ....
   B: I don't think so. ....

13 **Read and rewrite in the passive where necessary.**

1 We keep paper and extra stationery in the white cupboard, next to the photocopier.
2 We need to recycle tins and bottles. The office 'green team' have put special bins in the kitchen.
3 We could reuse printed paper. We can cut it into squares and use the blank side for notes.
4 The office canteen provides free snacks and refreshments at lunchtime.
5 We should wash all cups and plates before we leave the office.
6 We may keep plants next to our desks, but not on them.
7 We send regular memos by email.

OFFICE MEMO

Just to make our lives a bit easier …

1 *Paper and extra stationery are kept in the white cupboard, next to the photocopier.*

2 ....

3 ....

4 ....

5 ....

6 ....

7 ....

J. S. HARDY

> **Look!**
>
> Some verbs take two objects:
> *give, tell, send, show, bring, offer, pay*
> *Tom gave me the CD.*
> *The CD was given to me by Tom.*
> *I was given the CD by Tom.*

14 **Rewrite the sentences in the active.**

1 The last World Cup Final was watched by millions of people.
Millions of people *watched the last World Cup Final.* ....

2 The school play has been directed by Ms Fowler for the last three years.
Ms Fowler ....

3 Ben Adams is going to be replaced by John Larkin in the next series.
John Larkin ....

4 Tickets can be bought online.
You ....

5 The Olympic Games will be shown live on TV.
They ....

6 The school trip was cancelled because of bad weather.
The Headteacher ....

7 All the students have been invited to the music concert.
They ....

8 Personal items can be stored in the lockers.
You ....

15 **Read the information.**

> **By or with?**
> - We use *by* to introduce the agent.
> - We use *with* to introduce the means that is used to do something.
>
> *The cake was baked by Sandra.*
> (Sandra is the agent)
>
> *The cake was decorated with flowers.*
> (the flowers are the objects that were used to decorate the cake, not the agent)
> - Only use the agent when it is absolutely necessary.

16 **Complete with *by* or *with*.**

1 The instructions were given ...*by*........... the management.
2 The table will be covered .... a white cloth.
3 The treasure was found .... two local fishermen.
4 The bill can be paid .... a credit card.

5 The menu has been prepared .... a famous chef.
6 All the books were put into boxes .... the students.
7 The door cannot be opened .... this key.
8 The jam is made................ strawberries from our garden.

17 **Read the information.**

> **It is (said) that ...**
> When we want to talk about what people say / think / believe / know / claim, etc in general, we use the following form in the passive:
> *It is said / thought / believed / known etc that ...*
>
> **Active:** *People say that he is a good doctor.*
> **Passive:** *It is said that he is a good doctor.*
> **Active:** *They know that she loves animals.*
> **Passive:** *It is known that she loves animals.*

18 **Complete the sentences.**

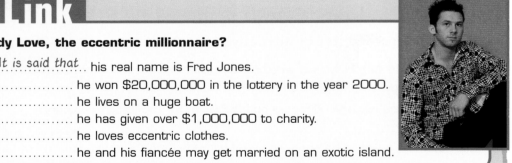

TeenLink

Who's Freddy Love, the eccentric millionnaire?

1 (say) *It is said that*... his real name is Fred Jones.
2 (believe) .... he won $20,000,000 in the lottery in the year 2000.
3 (claim) .... he lives on a huge boat.
4 (report) .... he has given over $1,000,000 to charity.
5 (know) .... he loves eccentric clothes.
6 (think) .... he and his fiancée may get married on an exotic island.

19 **Rewrite the sentences in the passive as in the example.**

1 We know that exercise can fight stress.
   It is known that exercise can fight stress.
2 People think that the thief has already left the country.
   ....
3 They report that we are going to have a very cold winter.
   ....
4 People say that the new sports centre is excellent.
   ....
5 They claim that the buildings were damaged in the earthquake.
   ....
6 We expect that the concert will be a success.
   ....

20 **Complete with *one* word.**

A block of flats on 21 Pine Street ¹ ....*was*..... damaged by fire last Tuesday afternoon. ² .... is believed that the fire started in a first-floor flat. The flat was ³ .... redecorated at the time by a local firm of builders. The building had already ⁴ .... evacuated before the fire brigade arrived. Unfortunately, most of the building ⁵ .... already been damaged before the fire ⁶ .... put out.

The men who were redecorating the first-floor flat that morning have ⁷ .... found and now they ⁸ .... being questioned ⁹ .... the police. The exact details ¹⁰ .... not known but it is ¹¹ .... that the fire started when one of the workers threw a lit cigarette next to a bottle of spirit. Repairs will ¹² .... made, but it will be a long time before the residents can go back to their homes.

Writing practice

21 **Read and write the *TeenLink* article. Use the passive.**

TeenLink

Indiana Jones trivia

1 The character of Indiana Jones / create / by George Lucas.
2 The adventurous professor / name / 'Indiana Smith' at first.
3 Indiana Jones / play / by the actor Harrison Ford in all four films.
4 The first film, *'Raiders of the Lost Ark'*, / follow / by *'Indiana Jones and the Temple of Doom'*.
5 In the third film, *'Indiana Jones and the Last Crusade'*, / Indiana's father / play / by Sean Connery.
6 The fourth film, *'Indiana Jones and the Kingdom of the Crystal Skull'*, / produce / nineteen years after the third film.

TeenLink

1 *The character of Indiana Jones was created by George Lucas.*
....
2 ....
....
3 ....
....
4 ....
....
5 ....
....
6 ....
....

12 Causative

'Have / get something done'

TeenLink

Hair Fashions in Ancient Egypt

Do you spend hours styling your hair in the morning? If you had been an Ancient Egyptian, things would have been different. Read about hair fashions of that time and find out why …

In ancient Egypt, common people had their hair cut short.

Rich Egyptians had hairdressers to look after their hair. They had it washed and perfumed very often. Both men and women wore wigs for formal occasions. These wigs were made from human hair or wool.

Priests had their heads shaved to honour their gods. This was also a sign of cleanliness.

Children had their heads shaved, too, except for long, thin strands of hair on the side of their head. This was in honour of the god Horus – he had worn his hair like that when he was a child.

1 **Complete the table.**

Causative	
Present simple	He has his car serviced every year.
Present continuous	He is .... his car serviced at the moment.
Past simple	He .... his car serviced yesterday.
Past continuous	He was .... his car serviced at 11 a.m.
Present perfect simple	He has .... his car serviced.
Past perfect simple	He .... had his car serviced before he went away.
will	He will have his car .... soon.
going to	He is going to .... his car serviced next week.
Modals	He should / might have his car serviced soon.

2 **Read the information.**

> **Causative**
>
> **Form**
>
> *To have* + object + past participle
>
> We form the causative with the verb *to be* in the appropriate tense or form followed by the object and the past participle of the verb we want to use.
>
> *George had his teeth cleaned at the dentist's yesterday.*
>
> *Have you had your house redecorated? It looks very nice.*
>
> *They won't have their washing machine repaired. They'll buy a new one.*
>
> • We can also use the verb *get* instead of *have*.
>
> *We got the parcels delivered on time.*
>
> **Use**
>
> We use the causative
>
> • to talk about services we receive from other people, usually professionals.
>
> *Anna washed her hair.*
>
> (active – Anna did this herself)
>
> *Anna had her hair washed at the hairdresser's.*
>
> (causative – someone else did this for her)
>
> • to talk about something bad that happened to someone.
>
> *Sam had his bike stolen.*
>
> *I had my car towed away because I had parked on a double yellow line.*
>
> When we need to say who performed the action we use *by*, as in the passive.
>
> *The producer of the play had the costumes designed by a famous fashion designer.*

3 **Circle the correct answer.**

1 I'm sorry, I can't do anything about the central heating myself, but I am going to repair it / **have it repaired** tomorrow.

2 John's washed Dad's car / **had Dad's car washed**. I think he's done a good job.

3 I've just **had my hair cut** / cut my hair by Jean Charles. Do you like it?

4 She doesn't know how to sew a button on. She always **has her clothes repaired** / repairs her clothes by someone else.

5 This meal is delicious. Did you make it / **have it made** yourself?

6 We are redecorating / **having our flat redecorated** so we are staying at a hotel for a few days.

7 **I clean my house** / I have my house cleaned once a week. I can't afford to pay someone else to do it.

8 If you can't read this, you might need to test your eyes / **have your eyes tested**.

4 **Complete with the correct form of *have*.**

1 Your hair is too long. I think you ....*should have*.... it cut next week. (should)

2 He has cream coloured carpets at home and he .... them cleaned twice a year. (present simple)

3 We .... the new printer installed when the power was cut off. (past continuous)

4 I'm so excited! I .... my book published! ('*going to*' future)

5 I can't come tomorrow. I .... my new sofa delivered. (present continuous)

6 The brakes on my bike were broken so I .... them replaced. (present perfect)

7 John had an accident last week and he .... his leg put in a plaster cast. (past simple)

8 I don't know how to do this myself, so I .... it done by someone else. ('*will*' future)

5 Rewrite the sentences in the causative form.

1 The shop is delivering my new bike today.
I 'm having my new bike delivered today. .

2 Your jacket needs to be dry cleaned.
You ....

3 My uncle's firm has designed their new offices.
They ....

4 They'll make a new wardrobe for our bedroom.
We ....

5 They replaced my mobile phone immediately.
I ....

6 Someone should service the air conditioning units before they use them.
They ....

7 The dog was examined by the vet.
We ....

8 The photographer is going to take her photo.
She ....

6 Complete with the causative.

1 **A:** Did .... your sister ... have ... her house ... decorated ... professionally? (decorate, past simple)
B: No, she .... it .... She did it herself. (not decorate, past simple).

2 **A:** .... we .... a satellite dish .... ? (install, 'going to')
B: Yes, we are. But we .... it before June. (not install, 'going to')

3 **A:** Your hair looks beautiful. .... you .... ? (cut, present perfect)
B: No, I haven't. I .... it .... at the hairdresser's. (style, present perfect)

4 **A:** .... you usually .... the carpets .... ? (clean, present simple)
B: No, I .... them .... professionally. I clean them myself. (not clean, present simple)

5 **A:** My teeth look yellow! .... them .... ? (whiten, 'should')
B: No, you .... them .... You need to brush them more often! (whiten, not need)

6 **A:** .... you .... the flowers .... or will you take them yourself? (deliver, 'will')
B: No, I .... them .... I think it's better to take them myself. (not deliver, 'will')

7 Write causative sentences with *get*.

1 We've just bought an air conditioning unit. (install)
We need to get it installed. .

2 Her house always looks perfect. (clean)
She .... every day.

3 The computer works now. (repair)
I .... yesterday.

4 This oven isn't safe. (replace)
I'm going ....

5 She likes her hair short. (cut)
She .... every month.

6 These shoes are just the right size for me. (make)
I .... specially.

7 They've just bought a new computer desk. (deliver)
They .... tomorrow.

8 There's a hole in the roof. (fix)
You must .... before it rains.

8 Rewrite the sentences using the words given.

1 The optician checks my eyes every year. **have**
I have my eyes checked every year .

2 They have changed our locks. **had**
We ....

3 Someone broke a window in my car. **got**
I ....

4 They have groomed Anna's dog. **had**
Anna ....

5 He is going to redesign her garden. **redesigned**
She ....

6 The dentist removed my wisdom teeth. **had**
I ....

7 The mechanic is checking the brakes **having**
I ....

9 Match and write.

1	electrical repairs / do	architect
2	our eyes / test	dentist
3	houses / design	electrician
4	our hair / cut	tailor
5	our teeth / check	hairdresser
6	suits / make	optician
7	cars / service	waiter
8	food / serve	mechanic

1 *We have electrical repairs done by an electrician.*
2 ....
3 ....
4 ....
5 ....
6 ....
7 ....
8 ....

Writing practice

10 Read. Then write sentences in the causative.

From: 'Haven Sports Centre' To: G. Hardy

Subject: Monthly Newsletter

Work in progress!

Dear member,

As you all know, we [1] *are having the gym and sports facilities redone* . At the moment, they look a bit like a disaster area, but, trust me, they're going to look great in the end.

First of all, we [2] .... At the moment, we [3] ....
.... You'll be thrilled to learn that they will be power showers – just the extra boost you need after a good workout!

Next week we [4] .... in the changing rooms.

We [5] .... already .... and we are planning [6] .... by next weekend.

Finally, we [7] .... and all the carpets replaced.

We are looking forward to seeing you soon in our brand new gym!

Best wishes,

Tom O'Grady

Public Relations Manager

1 the gym and sports facilities / redo
2 the swimming pool / retile
3 the showers / replace
4 some more lockers / add
5 the new gym equipment / deliver
6 everything / install
7 the whole gym / redecorate

13 Adjectives, adverbs

Comparative and superlative forms

1 Complete the tables.

Adjective	Comparative	Superlative
smart	....	the smartest
mean	meaner	the ....
....	hotter	the hottest
noisy	noisier	the ....
intelligent	more................	the most intelligent
good	better	the best
bad	worse	the worst
many	more	the most
much	more	the most
a lot	more	the most
(a) little	less	the least

Adverb	Comparative	Superlative
seriously	.... seriously	most seriously
happily	more happily	.... happily
....	more comfortably	most comfortably
carefully	more	most carefully
well	better	best
badly	worse	worst
fast	faster	fastest
hard	harder	hardest
early	earlier	earliest
late	later	latest
far	farther / further	farthest / furthest

2 **Read the information.**

Adjectives

We use adjectives
- before a noun to add information about it.

She has a beautiful house.   This is a big car.
- after the verb to be to give information about the subject of the verb

He is tall.   This building is new.
- after verbs of the senses (*e.g. look, seem, sound, smell, taste, feel*)

She looks young for her age.
This perfume smells wonderful.

Comparative form of adjectives
- (1–2 syllable adjective) -er than

Tom is taller than Nick.
- more (2+ syllable adjective) than

He is more intelligent than you.

Use

We use the comparative form to compare two people, animals, objects or situations between them.
Dan is older than I am.
Your joke was funnier than mine.
The film was more interesting than I had expected.

Superlative form of adjectives
- the (1–2 syllable adjective) -est

Tom is the tallest boy in his class.
- the most (2 + syllable adjective)

He is the most intelligent person I know.

Spelling rules for adjectives → page 141.
Some adjectives form the comparative and superlative irregularly. They are listed in the tables on page 90.

Use

We use the superlative form to compare one person, animal, object or situation with a number of others. With the superlative, we single out this person (animal, etc) from the rest because it has the quality that the adjective describes to the highest degree.
She is the fastest runner in her team.
Fred is the youngest in his family.
This is the most expensive pair of jeans in the shop.
This is the silliest thing you've ever done.

Adverbs

We use adverbs
- to give information about how something is done (adverbs of manner), when it is done (adverbs of time) or where something is (adverbs of place).
- Adverbs of manner are formed by adding the ending -ly to the adjective. Some adverbs are formed irregularly (e.g. *good–well*).

The adverb goes
- after a verb that doesn't have an object or after the object

She plays tennis well. They opened slowly.
- before an adjective or participle that is used as an adjective

It is terribly easy to do this.
The engine is carefully designed.

Comparative form of adverbs
- more (2 + syllable adverbs or adverbs that end in -ly) than

He played more carefully than his brother.

Superlative form of adverbs
- the most (2+ syllable adverbs or adverbs that end in -ly)

It was the most beautifully wrapped present I had ever seen.
Spelling rules for adverbs → page 141.
Some adverbs form the comparative and superlative irregularly. They are listed in the tables on page 90.

Use

We use the comparative and superlative forms of adverbs in the same way that we use the comparative and superlative forms of adjectives.
She writes more neatly than you do.
They behaved the most irresponsibly of all.

Please note that the adverb *far* has two comparative and superlative forms
- We use *far – farther – farthest* when we talk about actual distance and *far – further – furthest* when we are using the adverb figuratively.

He lives farther away from the school than me.
This is the furthest we can help you.

3 **Circle the correct answer.**

1 Peter has a very (good)/ well memory.
2 He walked slow / slowly because he had hurt his knee.
3 This isn't a funny / funnily joke.
4 Are you talking serious / seriously?
5 Lucy paints beautiful / beautifully.
6 Please play quiet / quietly. Your dad's sleeping.
7 That's a wise /wisely decision.
8 Drive careful / carefully, please.
9 Put on a warm / warmly jacket. It's cold outside.
10 She was extreme / extremely interested in what I had to say.

4 **Complete with an adjective or adverb.**

1 You have to do this job very ..*carefully*..
   (careful)
2 He was wearing a ..*trendy*.. T-shirt.
   (trendy)
3 In fairy tales people always live ....
   ever after. (happy)
4 She is a very .... girl. (polite)
5 I didn't sleep very .... last night.
   (good)
6 My hair feels very .... with this new
   shampoo. (soft)

7 He's speaking too .... I can't
   understand what he's saying. (quick)
8 The twins are rather .... for their
   age. (short)
9 The rain fell .... for about an hour.
   (heavy)
10 We ate quite .... at that restaurant.
   (cheap)
11 She's worked really .... all year.
   (hard)
12 They go to the gym .... (regular)

5 **Rewrite the sentence using the words given.**

1 The alligator made a slow movement. **moved**
   The alligator ..*moved slowly*.. .
2 When she came in, she had a happy smile on
   her face. **was**
   When she came in, she ....
3 We were comfortable in our seats. **sat**
   We ....
4 You have a healthy diet. **eat**
   You ....

5 His answer was correct. **answered**
   He ....
6 The children's games were noisy. **played**
   The children ....
7 The project was very successful in the end.
   finished
   They ....
8 He gave me a sad look. **looked**
   He ....

6 **Circle the correct answer.**

1 Our classroom is (warmer)/ more warmer than
   yours.
2 George tells more good / better jokes than
   Adam.
3 Her hair is lighter than / of mine.
4 She is a clever / cleverer student.
5 My great-grandfather is the oldest person
   in / than my family.
6 I am the tallest of / than all.

7 He plays better football than / from John.
8 You work more carefully / the most carefully
   than I do.
9 She gets up early / earlier than he does.
10 It was the strangest / stranger story he had
   ever heard.
11 He was the most / more advanced student in
   his class.
12 They have the / a best garden I've ever seen.

7 **Complete with the superlative.**

1 It was ....*the most exciting*........ thing that had ever happened to me. **exciting**
2 This is .... ticket I could find. **cheap**
3 Her speech was .... of all. **enjoyable**
4 The dining room is .... room in our house. **hot**
5 She is .... musician in her family. **talented**
6 He gave me .... present I have ever received. **good**
7 This must be .... exercise I have ever done. **hard**
8 This is .... part of the swimming pool, so be careful. **deep**
9 Although we were tired, my friend and I walked .... of all. **far**
10 I think he has .... singing voice in the class. **bad**

8 **Complete with the comparative or the superlative.**

1 Francis and Harry have worked ...*harder than*... anyone else on this project. **hard**
2 Let's sit in the garden; it's .... the house. **cool**
3 It was the .... thing he had ever done. **foolish**
4 Today the boys played .... the girls. **quietly**
5 Your score was .... in the class. Well done! **high**
6 This is .... I have ever had my hair cut. **short**
7 A pot of yogurt is a .... snack .... a donut. **healthy**
8 He's .... in his family. He never cleans up if he can avoid it! **lazy**
9 She dresses .... I do. **fashionably**
10 The apples were .... today .... they were last week. **cheap**

9 **Complete with the comparative or the superlative.**

TeenLink

Fact or fiction? by Harry Davis

Vroom!
The cheetah is [1] ...*the fastest*... (fast) animal on land. *It's a fact. A cheetah can reach a speed of 110 km an hour (and it doesn't need any fuel!)*

The snail is [2] .... (slow) animal in the world.
Don't know for a fact, but I'm working on it! I wonder how long a 'snail race' takes, though!

A hippo is [3] .... (fast) a man!
Believe it or not, it is! So don't think you can make fun of one and run...

See you later alligator!
Alligators can grow to 6 m long.
Fiction, but close. The [4] .... (long) alligator was 5 m 84 cm (recorded in 1900).

The [5] .... (rare) alligator is the Chinese alligator.
Fact. He's a beauty in the photo, isn't he? (He could use a dentist, though... .)

Big is beautiful
The African elephant is [6] .... (heavy) of all animals.
Fiction. The African elephant may be the winner on land but the blue whale is [7] .... (big) the African elephant. In fact, it is the [8] .... (large) animal in the world!

So long!
A giraffe can be [9] .... (tall) a tree.
Fact. A giraffe can grow up to 5.5 m. I hope it's not windy up there!

The Asiatic python is [10] .... (long) a boat.
I'd say fact and fiction, because it depends on how long the boat is! An Asiatic python can grow up to 10 m in length.

10 Read the information.

> **Other forms of comparison**
>
> *As...as,   not as / so ... as*
> When we make a comparison between two people, animals, objects, etc and we find that they are the same we use
> • *as* + adjective / adverb + *as*
> *I am as tall as you are.*
> *They worked as carefully as we did.*
> When we make a comparison and find that the people, animals, objects, etc we compare are not the same, we use
> • *not so / as* + adjective / adverb + *as*
> *The T-shirt isn't as expensive as the jeans.*
> *They don't stay up so late as you do.*
>
> *Less* + adjective / adverb (+ *than*)
> When we make a comparison we can use the word *less* instead of *more*.
> *Going out is more interesting than watching TV.*
> *Watching TV is less interesting than going out.*
>
> *Far / Much* + comparative
> We can use the words *far* and *much* before the adjective / adverb when we make a comparison to emphasise that the difference between the two people, animals, objects, etc we are comparing is great.
> *She is a far better cook than her mother.*
> *This is a much more comfortable sofa than the old one.*

11 Rewrite the sentences using *as ... as* or *not so / as ... as* and the word given.

1 Mary and Jenny are the same height.   **tall**
  Mary is as tall as Jenny.

2 A gazelle is fast, but a cheetah is faster.   **fast**
  A gazelle isn't as fast as a cheetah.

3 A bear is bigger than a fox.   **big**
  ....

4 My father and your father are the same age. **old**
  ....

5 She spoke more fluently than he did.   **speak**
  ....

6 Harry and Ben got the same marks in the test. **well**
  ....

7 Sandra is a healthy eater. So is Ann.   **healthily**
  ....

8 Today is hotter than yesterday.   **hot**
  ....

12 Rewrite the sentences using *less*.

1 Peter is more interested in Maths than Lucy.   Lucy is *less interested in Maths than Peter* .
2 Her photo was more beautiful than she was in real life.   In real life, she was ....
3 The lemon pie is sweeter than the cheesecake.   The cheesecake is ....
4 Plane journeys are more expensive than train journeys. Going by train is ....
5 William is more athletic than Ian.   Ian is ....
6 Speaking a foreign language is more difficult than reading it. Reading a foreign language is ....
7 Are dogs more intelligent than cats?   Are cats .... ?

13 Write comparative sentences with the word given.

1 Our team / played / bad / the other team (far)
  Our team played far worse than the other team.

2 A giraffe / tall / a cheetah (much)
  ....

3 This computer / is / powerful / my old computer (far)
  ....

4 I / feel / well / I did yesterday (much)
  ....

5 The last project / was / complicated / this one (far)
  ....

6 She / can skate / easily / she could last September (much)
  ....

7 The results of the test / were / bad / he / expected (far)
  ....

14 Choose the correct answer.

TeenLink

PC Game Review
'Changing Worlds 1' and 'Changing Worlds 2'
by Peter Hardy

First of all, I had never played 'Changing Worlds 1' before I played 'Changing Worlds 2'. I only got CW1 (that's 'Changing Worlds 1' for short ...) just to see if it was [1] ...*as boring*.... as CW2 but I was pleasantly surprised. CW1 was [2] .... than CW2. The characters were [3] .... and the adventures [4] .... than in CW2. CW1 also has [5] .... features I have ever seen in a game: you can make the hero look exactly like you! I just wonder why they didn't use this in CW2. I wouldn't go so far as to say that CW2 is the [6] .... game I have ever played, but it certainly comes close! One final word; although the graphics in CW1 aren't [7] .... in CW2, it still is [8] .... game.

1	a more boring	b boring	c as boring
2	a far interesting	b far more interesting	c much interesting
3	a more realistic	b most realistic	c much realistic
4	a more exciting	b not so exciting	c as exciting
5	a much better	b the far better	c the best
6	a far most boring	b most boring	c not so boring
7	a so advanced as	b as advanced	c more advanced
8	a the much better	b the better	c a far better

Writing practice

15 Write answers to the questions.

Use any form of the comparative or the superlative and the words suggested in your answer.

TeenLink

What's your opinion?

1 Which is the best pet? **(intelligent / good company)**
  I think the best pet is the .... *because it is* .... *than a* ....
  I also think it is the ....

2 Is football more interesting than tennis? **(popular / exciting)**
  ....
  ....

3 Which snack do you prefer: crisps or fruit? **(fattening / healthy)**
  ....
  ....

4 Who's your best friend? **(kind / understanding)**
  ....
  ....

Infinitive, gerund

Infinitive, gerund, '*too / (not) enough*', '*let / make*', '*would rather*', '*had better*', '*be used to*'

GLOBETROTTERS

- Are you tired of spending your holiday in the same place as everyone else?

- Are you bored with doing the same things year after year?

- Are you fed up with having to arrange everything yourself?

If you have answered '*yes*' to more than one of our questions, then:

Let us help you!

It's so easy to have the best holiday ever! Just ask us to do anything you like – we are used to dealing even with the most unusual requests!

We can make all the arrangements for the holiday of your dreams and offer lots of fresh ideas!

So, why wait? It's never too early to book your next holiday!

Come and see us, or give us a ring.
We look forward to seeing you!

GLOBETROTTERS TRAVEL AGENCY
21 Park Avenue.
Tel 332324 – 332345
Open Mon–Fri: 9 a.m.–9 p.m. Sat: 9 a.m.–5 p.m.

TRAVEL AGENCY

1 **Read the tables.**

Infinitive	
	It's easy to organise a holiday.
	He was pleased to see you.
	I'm too busy to watch TV.
	The house is big enough for all of us.
	She's decided to quit her job.
	My parents won't let me stay out later than 9 o'clock.
	They made me promise not to tell anyone.
	You'd better go to bed early.
	She might come over later.
	We'd rather eat at home tonight.
Gerund	Exercising is good for your health.
	He enjoys playing sports.
	I'm good at making things.
	She's used to working hard.

2 **Read the information.**

The infinitive

The infinitive is the basic form of a verb.

We use two forms of the infinitive

- the infinitive with '*to*'

I want to play a game.

- the infinitive without '*to*'

You'd better take a map with you.

Infinitive with '*to*'

We use the infinitive with '*to*'

- after these verbs:

advise	*expect*	*plan*
agree	*force*	*prefer*
allow	*forget*	*promise*
appear	*hate*	*refuse*
arrange	*help*	*seem*
ask	*hope*	*start*
begin	*learn*	*stop*
choose	*like*	*want*
continue	*manage*	*would like*
decide	*offer*	*would love*

They asked me to play the piano at the school concert.

I hope to see you soon.

She refuses to speak to him.

We would like to have lunch now, please.

- with the expression *too* + adjective / adverb + infinitive

She's too tired to go out tonight.

- The word '*too*' before an adjective / adverb gives a negative meaning to the sentence. It means 'more than it should be' or 'more than is necessary'.

He is too young to drive. (= he isn't allowed to drive because of his age)

- with the expression (*not*) adjective / adverb + *enough* + infinitive

It's warm enough to play outside.

I am not tall enough to reach the shelf.

- The word '*enough*' gives a positive meaning to the sentence. It means '*just as much as it should be*' or '*just as much as is necessary*'.

He's good enough to be a professional musician. (= he can be a professional musician if he wants to)

- with the expression *it* + *to be* + adjective + infinitive

It's nice to go on a short holiday when you can.

It was interesting to learn that the temple dated back to the 4th century BC.

- with the expression subject + *to be* + adjective + infinitive

They were happy to offer me the job.

I'm sorry to hear you are not well.

She's glad to be in the play.

Infinitive without '*to*'

We use the infinitive without '*to*'

- after the verbs *let* and *make*

I'll let you use my computer if you are careful.

My music teacher made me play the same piece three times.

- with the expression *would rather*

I'd rather do this on my own if you don't mind.

He'd rather stay in a hotel.

- with the expression *had better*

You'd better book the tickets as soon as possible.

She'd better not sing. She has an awful voice.

- after some modal verbs, such as *could, may, might, must, should*

He must call his parents right now.

You shouldn't wear my T-shirt without my permission.

- The verb *help* can be followed by both the infinitive with '*to*' and the infinitive without '*to*'. It makes no difference in meaning.

Will you help me carry these bags?

Will you help me to carry these bags?

3 **Write sentences.**

1	What / he / advise / you / do	(simple past)	*What did he advise you to do?*
2	I / hope / come back / soon	(simple present)	....
3	She / arrange / meet / us here	(present perfect)	....
4	you / promise / not tell / anyone	('*will*' future)	....
5	They / plan / move / to the country	(present continuous)	....
6	He / forget / lock / the door	(simple past)	....
7	I / not expect / see / you here	(past continuous)	....
8	I / like / meet / your friends	('*would*')	....

4 **Join the sentences. Use the word given.**

1	Katie is young. She can't stay at home on her own.	*Katie is too young to stay at home on her own.*	**too**
2	It's still early. I can cancel the tickets.	*It's early enough to cancel the tickets.*	**enough**
3	I'm tired. I can't cook dinner tonight.	....	**too**
4	He is clever. He won't make any mistakes.	....	**too**
5	The suitcase is big. It can hold your clothes and mine.	....	**enough**
6	It's cold. Let's not go out.	....	**too**
7	I'm not hungry. I don't want to have dinner now.	....	**enough**
8	She trains hard. She may win the competition.	....	**enough**

5 **Rewrite the underlined sentences. Use the word given.**

Read Aunt Agatha's postcard to Peter and Lucy. Rewrite the sentences.

Dear Jane, George, Peter and Lucy,

I am having a terrible time here. First of all, [1] my bed is too uncomfortable to sleep in.

[2] It is too hot to do any sightseeing. The prices at the shops are shocking! It seems [3] I'm not rich enough to buy anything! The waves are very rough. [4] I'm not brave enough to swim in the sea and the hotel swimming pool is full of young people. I don't think [5] it is clean enough to go in. As for the hotel itself, [6] it is too noisy to sleep in the evening. There's a disco every night! And the food doesn't look good. I'm sure [7] it isn't safe enough to eat. I really can't understand your cousin Betty! She says that she is having a fantastic time!

I am looking forward to returning to the comfort of my own home,

Love, Aunt Agatha

1	My bed *isn't comfortable enough* .... to sleep in.	**comfortable**
2	It isn't .... to do any sightseeing.	**cool**
3	I'm .... to buy anything!	**poor**
4	I'm .... to swim in the sea.	**scared**
5	It's .... to go in.	**dirty**
6	It isn't .... to sleep.	**quiet**
7	It's .... to eat.	**unsafe**

6 **Complete the sentences.**

1 I hear you got a very good school report. I'm pleased about it.
I'm ..*pleased to hear*.................. you got a very good school report.

2 We go for a walk in the countryside. It's refreshing.
It's .... for a walk in the countryside.

3 I won top prize in the competition. I'm happy about it.
I was .... top prize in the competition.

4 They want to go out for a meal. It's too late.
It's .... for a meal.

5 They found the front door unlocked. They were surprised about it.
They were .... the front door unlocked.

6 Everything is OK. She will be relieved about that.
She will be ....
everything is OK.

7 We watch TV all day. It's boring.
It's .... TV all day.

7 **Rewrite the sentences. Use the word given.**

1 I prefer to go home now.   **rather**
I'd rather go home now.
....

2 You should listen to your mother.   **better**
....

3 They think it is better to go to the cinema.   **rather**
....

4 She needs to eat more healthily.   **better**
....

5 We should be more careful in the future.   **better**
....

6 He prefers to wait for the bus.   **rather**
....

8 **Complete with *make* or *let* and the words given.**

1 John doesn't like going to bed early but his mum ..*makes him go to bed*...... at 9 o'clock on weekdays.
At the weekend, she .... any time he likes.   **him / go to bed (x2)**

2 My brother .... when I go into his room, but he .... when I want.   **me / knock; me / use his computer**

3 Julia's mum .... fruit every day. On the other hand, she ....
eat anything she wants for dinner.   **her / eat (x2)**

4 I love TV, but my parents only .... until 8 o'clock. After that they ....
.... and do something else.   **me / watch; me / turn it off**

9 **Complete with the infinitive with or without 'to'.**

1 I prefer ....*to work*.......... alone. (work)
2 I'm very pleased .... you. (meet)
3 It's nice .... someone to help in the shop. (have)
4 Samantha would like .... to you for a minute. (speak)
5 We'd rather not .... a new car if our old one can be repaired. (buy)
6 The coach made the team .... they could win! (believe)
7 You'd better .... to a doctor about your headaches. (talk)
8 He's too polite .... a fuss about the bad service. (make)

10 **Read the information.**

The gerund

The gerund is formed by adding -ing to the basic form of the verb.

We use the gerund

- as a noun. It can be the subject or object of another verb and it can take an adjective.

Travelling by plane is faster than taking the car.
Careful planning is necessary in this job.

- after some expressions that end with a preposition:

  be afraid of, be interested in, be bad at, be keen on, be bored with, be sorry for, be crazy about, be tired of, be fed up with, have difficulty in, be fond of, look forward to, be good at

I'm sorry for breaking your vase.
She's keen on knitting.

- after the verbs:

  avoid, keep, deny, mind, dislike, remember, enjoy, stop, finish, suggest

He has finished talking.
I don't mind waiting.

- after the expressions:

  can't help, it's no good, can't stand, it's not worth, it's no use

It's not worth repairing this TV. You'd better buy a new one.
Sorry, I can't help laughing. It was such a funny story!

- with the expression *be/get + used + to + doing* (something)

NB: Do not confuse this expression with the expression *used + to do + (something)*.

I used to live in London. (= it is something I did in the past but not now)
I am used to living in London. (= at first I found it hard / didn't like it, but it's OK now)

Gerund or infinitive?

These verbs can be followed by either the gerund or the infinitive without changing their meaning:

begin, hate, continue, prefer, like, start, love
Suddenly, it started to rain.
Suddenly, it started raining.
I prefer sleeping with a light on.
I prefer to sleep with a light on.

These verbs can be followed by either the gerund or the infinitive but the meaning of the sentence changes:

stop, remember, try
She remembered to take her bag.
(She took it with her.)
She remembered taking her bag.
(She recalls the fact that she had her bag with her.)
They stopped reading this magazine.
(They don't do this anymore.)
They stopped to read this magazine.
(They stopped in order to read this magazine.)
I tried to fix the bike myself.
(I put some effort into it.)
I tried fixing the bike myself.
(I made an attempt just to see if I could do it.)

11 **Complete with the gerund.**

1 Mum enjoys ....*cooking*........ for my friends. (cook)

2 .... is good for you. (walk)

3 Keep .... I'm listening. (talk)

4 Are you interested in ....? (skate)

5 They are very good at .... things. (fix)

6 She isn't used to .... up so late. (stay)

7 I'm fed up with ....! I need a break! (study)

8 It's no use .... him what to do. (tell)

9 She can't stand .... to this kind of music. (listen)

10 Will you do the ....? I'm too tired. (wash up)

12 Rewrite the sentences using the words given.

TeenLink

From London with love ...

We've asked some visitors to tell us what they like about London.

1 Walking everywhere is easy because it is a flat city!   **walk**

It's easy to walk everywhere because it is a flat city!

(Lee, 24, from San Francisco)

2 Spending a whole day in Kew Botanical gardens was amazing!   **spend**

....

(Victoria, 40, from Madrid)

3 It's so easy to travel by Tube.   **travelling**

....

(Yiannis, 31, from Athens)

4 Shopping in Bond Street was great, but too expensive!   **shop**

....

(Annelise, 20, from Vienna)

5 It was a great experience to visit Madame Tussaud's!   **visiting**

....

(Ian and Michael, 11, from Australia)

6 It's impossible to see everything in the Natural History Museum in one visit.   **seeing**

....

(Carlo, 54, from Genova)

13 Read the first part of the story and complete. Use *used to* and the infinitive.

TeenLink

Tom and Keira Lewis two years ago.

Tom and Keira Lewis [1] *used to live* .. in the city a few years ago. Tom worked for a big company and Keira [2] .... (be) a lawyer. Both of them [3] .... (work) long hours. Some weekdays they only [4] .... (see) each other when they got up in the morning, and when they went to bed at night. This also meant that they [5] .... (not / see) their friends very often. They [6] .... (say): 'One day, we'll sell everything and go and live in the country!'

14 Read the second part of the story and complete. Use *be used to* and the gerund.

Tom's pigs

Which is exactly what they did! One year ago, they sold their flat in the city and bought a small farm in the country. [1] *Are they used to living* (live) a simpler life? 'Absolutely!' says Tom. Things weren't easy from the beginning, though. Both of them [2] .... (work) hard, but they [3] .... (not / get) up at dawn! Keira says: 'In the city I had my flat cleaned and my clothes ironed. I [4] .... (do) everything myself now, but it took me some time.' Tom says that although he has always been fit, he [5] .... (not / work) so hard with his hands. One thing that hasn't changed? 'I always listen to loud music when I work' says Tom. 'My pigs [6] .... (eat) their food to sounds of '*Hits of the '90s*'. I think they look happier when I play this CD!'

15 Choose and complete. Some of the verbs can take both the infinitive and the gerund so write both answers.

> work ~~rain~~ see run ~~worry~~ invite think

1 It started ..*to rain / raining*.. so we had to cancel the game.
2 It's not worth ..*worrying*...... about the test. I'm sure you have done well.
3 She can't stand .... for that company anymore. She's going to quit.
4 He continued .... although he was in pain because he wanted to finish the race.
5 They love .... people for dinner. They're both great cooks, too.
6 I didn't tell anyone, but I couldn't help .... that I had made a mistake.
7 We look forward to .... you at the school fete. I hope you can come.

16 Complete with the gerund or the infinitive.

1 I've stopped ..*eating*........ junk food at work. I eat fruit or a salad instead. (eat)
2 What's the TV remote control doing in the cupboard? I don't remember .... it there. (put)
3 I tried .... you about ten times, but you never answered your mobile! (call)
4 Why don't you try .... this cream? It might be good for you. (use)
5 Remember .... the tickets tomorrow. They might sell out if you wait too long. (buy)
6 Have you ever stopped .... if what you are doing is right? (think)
7 I'll try .... the essay tonight, but I might not be able to. (finish)

17 Complete with the gerund or the infinitive (with or without 'to').

1 The five-year-old boy denied ..*breaking*..... his neighbour's window. (break)
2 I'm fed up with .... (do) all the cleaning myself. You should .... (help), too!
3 Mum, I promise .... (do) all my homework tomorrow if you let me .... (go) to the cinema tonight.
4 It's nice .... (look) at old photos. Mum and Dad used .... (be) so young in these!
5 It's no use .... (talk) to him. He's fed up with people .... (tell) him what to do.
6 We are having some difficulty .... (find) your order right now. Would you mind .... (come) back later?
7 You can't make her .... (listen) to you. Try .... (listen) to her for once!

18 Rewrite the sentences using the words given.

1 Our teacher doesn't let us use calculators in class. **allow**
  Our teacher .... calculators in class.
2 She is very excited about meeting her favourite TV star. **forward**
  She is .... her favourite TV star.
3 Swimming in the sea is refreshing. **swim**
  It's .... in the sea.
4 I didn't want to laugh, but he forced me to – he was so funny! **made**
  He .... – he was so funny!
5 He was too young to see the film. **old**
  He .... the film.
6 She prefers to buy fruit and vegetables in the local market. **rather**
  She .... in the local market.
7 You should go to bed early tonight – you look tired. **better**
  You .... – you look tired.

19 Circle the correct answer.

TeenLink

What bugs you?

I'm not very keen [1] *on going* to the cinema. I [2] .... wait for a film to come out on DVD. I think it's more fun [3] .... my friends over and watch a DVD together at home, because we [4] .... talk, make jokes or rewind a scene as many times as we like! At the cinema we are not [5] .... to talk at all!
Leanne, 14

I've got millions of hobbies, but I'm not interested [6] .... any sports at all. My dad thinks it's very strange because he [7] .... a professional footballer and my granddad has always been [8] .... keeping fit – he played lots of sports when he was younger. He still enjoys [9] .... for a swim at the local sports centre every day and he's ninety years old! As for me, I'm quite happy[10] .... my bike for exercise.
Kenny, 12

1	a to go	(b on going)	c on go
2	a like	b 'm fond of	c 'd rather
3	a invite	b to invite	c of inviting
4	a can	b enjoy	c prefer
5	a fed up with	b allowed	c let
6	a to do	b doing	c in doing
7	a used to be	b was used to be	c was used to being
8	a like	b crazy about	c good
9	a going	b to go	c the going
10	a of riding	b in riding	c to ride

Writing practice

20 Read and write.

Write a few sentences about yourself and the things you do. Use the words in bold in your answers.

1	**enjoy**	I enjoy watching TV with my friends because we can talk about the things we see.
2	**would love**	....
3	**don't mind**	....
4	**good at**	....
5	**let**	....
6	**listening**	....
7	**I'm happy to**	....
8	**It's hard to**	....

Use your English (Units 11–14)

1 Change the sentences into the passive. Only add the agent if necessary.

1 Someone locked the door.
The door was locked.

2 Ian is going to interview James Watson.
....

3 They are redecorating the café.
....

4 My brother will deliver the parcel.
....

5 Someone has repaired the fridge.
....

6 People say that she was a famous actress.
....

7 They service their car once a year.
....

8 They should keep this plant indoors.
....

9 Adam gave me this book.
....

10 We covered the sofa with an old sheet.
....

2 Complete.

TeenLink

On the 10th of this month a music concert [1] *will be given* (give – *'will'* future) at our school.
It [2] .... (organise – present continuous) by the school music department and Mark
Richards, the famous pop star, who used to be a student at our school. Most of the tickets
[3] .... already .... (sell – present perfect), so if you want to be there, hurry
before the last ones [4] .... (snap up – present simple)! Also, [5] .... (say –
present simple) that Mark will not be the only famous person in the concert. His old group,
'The Shout', [6] .... (ask – present perfect) to perform a few of their songs and
[7] .... (believe – present simple) they have agreed! Of course the money
[8] .... (collect – present continuous) for charity – it [9] .... (give – *'going to'*)
to the local animal shelter.

3 Rewrite the sentences in the causative.

1 Someone must replace the broken window.
You must have the broken window replaced.

2 Someone had dry-cleaned Nick's suit for the party.
Nick ....

3 A man delivers our lunch to the office at 1 p.m. every day.
We ....

4 The hairdresser has cut my hair short.
I' ....

5 Someone should repair Ken's watch.
Ken ....

6 The dentist checked Mary's teeth last month.
Mary ....

7 When I phoned Sue, someone was installing her new computer.
When I phoned Sue, she ....

8 Someone must fix his TV.
He ....

104

4 **Complete with the correct form of the adjective or adverb.**

Dennis Grant's new film, *Ted's Worst Fear*, is finally out next Friday! We have all been looking forward to it for some time, so shall we rush to book our tickets?

We all know that Ted is played by one of 1 *the most famous* (famous) Hollywood actors of all time. He has had a 2 .... (long) and 3 .... (far / successful) career than any other film star. In fact, he has just been named as 4 .... (talented) comedy actor of our times by *Cinema Fan* magazine, and that means something. Surely his new film should be at least as 5 .... (good) his last one?

Well, I'm not so sure. In his role as Ted, he is 6 .... (less / funny) we might expect. This may be because the film has 7 .... (boring) dialogue and plot in the world! Although it is clear that Dennis tries 8 .... (hard) in his last film, he just can't make it work.

I'm sure that, reading this, you will feel 9 .... (disappointed) as I did when I saw this film, but believe me, you'll have a 10 .... (far / good) time if you stay at home and watch TV!

5 **Complete with the gerund or the infinitive.**

1 I'm sorry for ... *breaking* .... your glasses. It was an accident.   (break)
   It's OK. I was tired of ... *wearing* .... the same pair all the time, anyway.   (wear)
2 We'll be really happy .... your mum next weekend.   (see)
   Thanks. She's looking forward to .... you, too.   (meet)
3 .... late at night is bad for your health.   (eat)
   But I hate .... to bed with an empty stomach!   (go)
4 Did you manage .... your room yesterday?   (clean)
   Yes, I did but I was too tired .... anything else after that.   (do)
5 Would you mind .... the door, please?   (close)
   I'm sorry, I have to .... some boxes in first.   (carry)
6 We'd love .... our holiday in the same place next year.   (spend)
   It's good .... that you've had such a good time.   (hear)
7 Did you remember .... the milk?   (bring)
   Yes, here it is. I stopped .... some on my way home.   (buy)
8 We've arranged .... swimming tomorrow.   (go)
   The water isn't warm enough .... yet.   (swim)
9 How about .... out for dinner tonight?   (go)
   I'm tired. I'd rather .... at home and order a pizza.   (stay)
10 Don't let Mike .... any more cake. He's too greedy!   (eat)

Now you can ...

✔ Use the passive to focus on an action and make your speech more formal.
Five hundred new trees have been planted in the area that was damaged by fire last year.
All dishes are prepared with olive oil.

✔ Talk about services you receive.
We had the kitchen redecorated last month.
She's has her watch repaired.

✔ Make comparisons in a variety of ways.
Emily isn't as tall as her sister.
The book is far better than the film.
Walking is less tiring than just standing still.

✔ Use the gerund and the infinitive forms of the verb appropriately.
He's too young to stay at home on his own.
It's not worth repairing this old clock. Just get a new one.

15 Reported speech

Reported statements, commands, requests and questions

TeenLink

Speechless!
by Lucy Hardy

That's what I was when I met my favourite film star in person! I was buying a magazine with my friend, Sophie, when I saw Daniel Radcliffe standing next to me. I almost fainted! Sophie, who's better at these things than I am, asked Daniel if he could give us his autograph and Daniel said he'd be glad to. He had some photos on him, but he didn't have a pen so he asked me if I had one. I was so thrilled to see him that although I opened and closed my mouth, no words came out! Daniel asked if I was OK and Sophie said that I usually didn't know when to stop talking. She added that it was the first time she had seen me speechless. Daniel laughed, signed the photos for us and waved goodbye. I don't know how long I just stood there, unable to move. I told Sophie that I couldn't believe what had just happened. Well, at least I've got the photo to prove it!

1 Complete the table.

Direct speech	Reported speech
Christina said, 'I know him.'	Christina .... (that) she knew him.
Dan said to me, 'I answered the phone.'	Dan told me (that) he had .... the phone.
Lucy told Sophie, 'I can't believe it!'	Lucy told Sophie (that) she couldn't .... it.
The policeman said to the driver, 'Stop the car!'	The policeman ordered the .... to stop the car.
She said to us, 'Don't be late, please.'	She asked us not .... late.'
I said, 'Where did you find this?'	I asked where he had .... it.
My friend asked, 'Did you see the last episode of the series yesterday?'	My friend asked (me) if / whether I had .... the last episode of the series the day before.

2 **Read the information.**

Direct speech

We use direct speech when we want to tell someone what a third person has said using the exact words. By doing this we 'quote' what this person has said.

We use a reporting verb and quotes (' '). The most common reporting verbs are *say* and *ask*.
Ed said, 'I play volleyball every week.'
They asked 'Where is the teacher's office?'

Reported speech

Statements

We use reported speech when we want to tell someone what a third person has said but without using the exact words.

We use a reporting verb but we do not use quotes. The most common reporting verbs in reported statements are *say* and *tell*. We can use the word that to introduce the reported sentence if we like.
He said, 'I'm having a good time.'
(direct speech)
He said (that) he was having a good time.
(reported speech)

What changes from direct to reported statements?

• The reporting verb.

Direct speech	Reported speech
John said, 'I am tired.'	John said (that) he was tired. (reporting verb without indirect object)
John said to me, 'I am tired.'	John told me (that) he was tired. (reporting verb with indirect object)

• Personal pronouns, object pronouns and possessive adjectives.
   All changes are made according to who is talking about whom. For example:

Direct speech	Reported speech
George said to me, 'I like you'. (subject pronoun) (object pronoun)	George told me he liked me.
Kate said, ' My room is a mess!' (possessive adjective)	Kate said (that) her room was a mess.

• Verb tenses.
   We change verb tenses when the reporting verb is in the past simple. We do this because we are now at a different point in time from when the actual words were spoken. For example:

Direct speech	Reported speech
Last Saturday, Peter said, 'I'm going to the cinema.'	Last Saturday Peter said (that) he was going to the cinema.

At the time we are speaking, Saturday is in the past.

We have to change the tense to show this.

You will find a table that shows how tenses change from direct to reported speech on page 108.

Direct speech	Reported speech
Present simple Harry said, 'Sam eats everything.'	**Past simple** Harry said (that) Sam ate everything.
Present continuous Anna said, 'I'm working late.'	**Past continuous** Anna said (that) she was working late.
Past simple Fiona said, 'It rained all day!'	**Past perfect simple** Fiona said (that) it had rained all day.
Past continuous Dan said, 'We were listening to music.'	**Past perfect continuous** Dan said (that) they had been listening to music.
When / while with past simple and past continuous Vicky said, 'I was cooking when the phone rang.'	**No change** Vicky said (that) she was cooking when the phone rang.'
Present perfect simple James said, 'I have read the book.'	**Past perfect simple** James said (that) he had read the book.
Present perfect continuous Nadia said, 'I've been studying all morning.'	**Past perfect continuous** Nadia said (that) she had been studying all morning.
Past perfect simple Tom said, 'We had already left.'	**No change** Tom said (that) they had already left.
Past perfect continuous Susan said, 'I had been running.'	**No change** Susan said (that) she had been running.
will David said, 'She'll call us.'	**would** David said (that) she would call them.
am / are / is going to Claire said, 'They're going to sing.'	**was / were going to** Claire said (that) they were going to sing.
Infinitive with or without to Ian said, 'It's silly not to go.'	**No change** Ian said (that) it was silly not to go.

Modal verbs

Direct speech	Reported speech
may / might Fred said, 'It may not be easy.'	**might** Fred said (that) it might not be easy.
can / could Chris said, 'You can leave.'	**could** Chris said (that) we could leave.
should Martha said, 'We should pay.'	**should** Martha said (that) they should pay.
must / have to Eddie said, 'The door must close.'	**had to** Eddie said (that) the door had to close.
ought to Mark said, 'I ought to do it.'	**ought to** Mark said (that) he ought to do it.

- Time expressions, adverbs of place and some verbs that show movement.
  Again, these changes are made to reflect the difference in time and place between direct speech (when the words were actually spoken) and reported speech (when and where the person who reports these words is at the moment).

Direct speech	Reported speech
now William said, 'I'm leaving now.'	**then** William said (that) he was leaving then.
today, tonight 'Julie said, 'It's hot tonight.'	**that day, that night** Julie said (that) it was hot that night.
yesterday Jack said, 'I saw Jools yesterday.'	**the day before / the previous day** Jack said (that) he had seen Jools the day before / the previous day.
last week / month / year Harry said, 'I talked to her last week.'	**the week / month / year before, the previous week / month / year** Harry said (that) he had talked to her the week before / the previous week.
tomorrow Oliver said, 'The concert is tomorrow.'	**the next day / the following day** Oliver said (that) the concert was the next day / the following day.
next week / month / year Jen said, 'I'll see you next year!'	**the following week / month / year** Jen said (that) she would see us the following year.
this / these + noun George said, 'This book is interesting.'	**that / those + noun , the + noun** George said (that) that book was interesting. George said the book was interesting.
this / these Paul said, 'These are very nice.'	**it / they** Paul said (that) they were very nice.
here Sylvia said, 'I live here.'	**there** Sylvia said (that) she lived there.
come Beth said, 'I'll come!'	**go** Beth said (that) she would go.

Other reporting verbs

There are various other reporting verbs we can use instead of *say* or *tell* depending on the meaning we want to add to the reported sentence. Here are some examples:

add
Adam said that he was happy to be there. He added that it was the first time he had ever visited their country.

point out
Sam pointed out that it was already too late to go out.

remark
Eleanor remarked that the new car wasn't as comfortable as the old one.

whisper, yell
Vicky whispered that we should all be quiet in the library.
Henry yelled that everything was OK down there.

3 **Complete with *said* or *told*.**

1 Ian ...*said*......... that he had bought the tickets.
2 They .... , 'It is a wonderful day.'
3 He .... to her, 'This is where I live.'
4 Paul .... her that the sports centre was closed.
5 You .... me that it was a good film.
6 My friends .... me, 'You're crazy to do this!'
7 Betty .... to her teacher, 'I haven't got a pen.'

┌─ **Look!** ──────────────────────────┐
│ Remember: │
│ **Direct speech**   **Reported speech** │
│ *He said, '... .'*   *He said (that) ... .* │
│ *He said to Nick, '... .'* *He told Nick (that) ... .* │
└──────────────────────────────────────┘

4 **Rewrite the sentences in reported speech.**

1 Kenneth said, 'I'll be at Jim's.'   *Kenneth said that he would be at Jim's.*
2 Tom said, 'Tina is waiting for me outside.'   ....
3 Fred said, 'I only watch TV at the weekend.'   ....
4 Mum said, 'The washing machine isn't working.'   ....
5 Evelyn said, 'I'm going to buy a new car.'   ....
6 Samantha said to us, 'I am twelve years old.'   ....
7 Joe said to his brother, 'I broke the window.'   ....
8 Dan said, 'I have ordered pizza.'   ....
9 Mark said to me, 'I've been painting my room.'   ....
10 Ryan said, 'We will have a great time at the party.'   ....

5 **Rewrite the sentences in reported speech.**

1 The teacher said to us, 'You should finish the project as soon as possible.'
The teacher told us that we should finish the project as soon as possible.

2 Dad said to my brother, 'You ought to be ashamed of what you've done!'
....

3 She said to him, 'You can stay as long as you like.'
....

4 They said, 'It may be a long time before you see the results.'
....

5 Michael said, 'We could go to the theatre together.'
....

6 Our coach said, 'We must win this game!'
....

7 Adrian said to me, 'You might have a chance to meet the President.'
....

6 **Circle the correct answer.**

1 Ian said that he would go to France next month / (the following month)
2 Fred asked, 'Will you give me a ring tomorrow / the next day?'
3 They said that they / these were the wrong books.
4 Peter said to Ian, 'Hi, I am here / there!'
5 Tina said that she had seen the dentist the month before / last month.
6 Lee told me that they kept all their junk in here / there.
7 When I met Kim, she said that Bob didn't look well today / that day.
8 I said, 'I'm going to look for a new job next week / the following week.'

7 **Rewrite the sentences in reported speech. Use the reporting verb given.**

I Pam: 'The picnic is tomorrow.' (point out)   *Pam pointed out that the picnic was the following day.*

2 Fred: 'We should all be very quiet.' (whisper) ....

3 Nick: 'These shoes look very uncomfortable.' (add) ....

4 Joe: 'We must wear our badges all the time. (remark) ....

5 Ben: 'No one is allowed to come in here!' (yell) ....

6 Ellie: 'They will visit us again next year.' (say) ....

7 Ron: 'I learned how to play tennis last year. (point out) ....

8 Tom: 'I didn't go out of the house yesterday.' (remark) ....

9 Maria: 'This is a horrible thing to happen.' (say) ....

10 Harry: 'I'm doing my homework now.' (add) ....

8 **Read the information.**

When we want to report whole paragraphs, we don't use a reporting verb before each sentence. We usually join sentences that are relevant with *and* or *because*. This way we only use a reporting verb in the first sentence.

He said that the museum was wonderful and that we should visit it one day.

She said she would have to leave early because she was very tired.

We also try to use as many different reporting verbs as we can to avoid repetition.

9 **Read. Then report what Mr Gordon said, using the words given.**

TeenLink

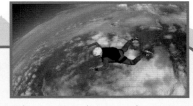

Mr Gordon, our PE teacher, has just returned from a skydiving holiday in America. Read all about his thrilling experience!

1 'Skydivers have to be eighteen or older.' (said) 'They should be very fit.' (and)

2 'The equipment can only weigh around 15 kilos.' (added)

3 'Each skydiver has two parachutes. One is the main canopy and the other is the reserve parachute.' (told me)

4 'At one point I was falling at a speed of 120 mph.' (said) 'At that speed I couldn't breathe.' (and)

5 'Skydivers don't suffocate' (pointed out) 'Their body absorbs oxygen through the skin at that pressure.' (because)

6 'I didn't land like a sack of flour as I had expected.' (remarked) 'The landing was quite smooth.' (and)

7 'It was a great experience!' (add) 'I'm looking forward to my next jump!' (and)

1 Mr Gordon *said that sky divers had to be eighteen or or older and that they should be very fit.*

2 He added that ....

3 Mr Gordon told me ....

....

4 ....

....

5 ....

....

6 ....

....

7 ....

....

....

10 Read the information.

Reported speech
Commands and requests

- In direct speech, we use the imperative to order someone to do something (command) or ask someone to do something (request).

What changes from direct to reported commands and requests?

- The verbs we use to introduce reported commands are *tell* and *order*. The verbs we use to report a request are *ask* and in some cases *beg* if it is appropriate. We do not use *say*.

Direct speech	Reported speech
The guard said to us, 'Stop!'	The guard ordered us to stop.
The parking attendant said to him, 'Don't park here!'	The parking attendant told him not to park there.
Oliver said to Mary, 'Please close the door'.	Oliver asked Mary to close the door.

The verb form

- When we report a command or request the imperative changes into the infinitive.

Direct speech	Reported speech
The captain said to his crew, 'Start getting ready!'	The captain ordered his crew to start getting ready.
Sandra said to them, 'Don't walk on the carpet with your shoes on!'	Sandra told them not to walk on the carpet with with their shoes on.

11 Choose the correct reporting verb and rewrite the sentences in reported speech.

1 Peter said to Lucy, 'Give me my MP3 player back!'   **told** / asked
  Peter told Lucy to give him his MP3 player back.
  ....

2 Kate said to me, 'Please don't tell anyone about it.'   **ordered** / **asked**
  ....

3 Tom said to Jen, 'Stop being so silly and listen to me!'   **told** / **asked**
  ....

4 The policeman said to the man, 'Don't move!'   **ordered** / **asked**
  ....

5 Beth said to Lucy, 'Call me back later, please.'   **told** / **asked**
  ....

6 Nick said to his father, 'Please lend me your camera!'   **ordered** / **asked**
  ....

7 The teacher said to us, 'Open your books to page 45.'   **told** / **asked**
  ....

8 Ryan said to her, 'Turn down the music, please.'   **told** / **asked**
  ....

9 The man said to the dog, 'Don't touch the food!'   **ordered** / **asked**
  ....

10 The sergeant said to the soldier, 'Come with me!'   **ordered** / **asked**
  ....

12 **Read the information.**

- Words like *please*, exclamation marks and any words we use to add colour or emphasis to direct speech are omitted in reported speech.

- Direct requests are made in different ways, but they are always reported the same way.
  'Could you do me a favour?'
  'Will you do me a favour?'
  She asked me to do her a favour.

13 **Rewrite the sentences using the words given.**

1 Mr Horton said to his son, 'Sit down and do your homework!' **ordered**
   Mr Horton *ordered his son to sit down and do* .... his homework.

2 Beth said to Peter, 'Could you bring me some paper?' **asked**
   Beth *asked Peter to bring her* .... some paper.

3 Denise said to her mum, 'Please let me go on the school trip.' **asked**
   Denise .... on the school trip.

4 Fred said to me, 'Will you put these bottles on the recycling bin?' **asked**
   Fred .... in the recycling bin.

5 Mr Hardy said to Lucy, 'Do what I say, young miss!' **told**
   Mr Hardy .... said.

6 Grandma Hardy said to Peter, 'Will you open the door, please?' **asked**
   Grandma Hardy .... the door.

7 Sue said to her brother, 'Lend me ten pounds, please.' **asked**
   Sue .... ten pounds.

14 **Read the information.**

Reported speech
Questions
What changes from direct to reported questions?

- The reporting verb.

The verbs we use to introduce reported questions are *ask, want to know* and *wonder*.

Direct speech	Reported speech
John said to me, 'Are you OK?'	John asked if I was OK.
She said, 'Who is that man?'	She wanted to know who that man was.
He said, 'Will it rain?'	He wondered if it would rain.

- Verb tenses and the structure of the sentence.

Verb tenses change in exactly the same way as in statements.
Reported questions follow the structure of statements.
Direct questions that begin with a verb are introduced with *if* or *whether*.
Direct questions that begin with a question word are introduced with the same question word.

Direct speech	Reported speech
Henry said, 'Are you waiting for me?'	Henry asked if / whether we were waiting for him.
Bea said, 'When was your birthday?'	Bea wanted to know when my birthday was.
Tom asked, 'Where did you find the keys?'	Tom asked where I had found the keys.

- Time expressions, adverbs of place and some verbs that show movement. These change in the same way as in statements.

15 Rewrite the questions in reported speech. Use the reporting verbs given.

1 **Alex**: 'Is it raining in Berlin?   **ask**
   Alex asked if it was raining in Berlin.

2 **Sam**: 'When are they going to finish?'   **want to know**
   ....

3 **Andy**: 'Did your brother win the race?'   **ask**
   ....

4 **Chris**: 'Where did you go last Saturday?'   **ask**
   ....

5 **Maria**: Does Ken have the right address?'   **wonder**
   ....

6 **Vicky**: 'Why have you packed your suitcase?'   **want to know**
   ....

7 **Kate**: 'How long has he been waiting?'   **wonder**
   ....

8 **Mr Saunders**: 'Have you fed the goldfish?'   **ask**
   ....

9 **Beth**: 'Did Mark stay at his aunt's?'   **want to know**
   ....

10 **Steve**: 'Were they watching TV?'   **ask**
   ....

16 Read and complete. Use reported speech.

1 'You are very bad tempered!'
2 'I don't want to speak to you!'
3 'You don't have to be my friend anymore.'
4 'Do you mean this?'
5 'I won't bother you in the future.'
6 'We've never fought like this before.'
7 'We had a fight like this last month!'
8 'Why are you behaving like a four-year-old?'
9 'Because you started it!'
10 'Oh, grow up Lucy!'

Peter: You look upset, Lucy. What's happened?

Lucy: I've had a terrible fight with Sophie. She said [1] *I was very bad tempered* and then she said
        [2] .... Then I said [3] .... and she asked
        [4] .... I said that [5] .... And then she said that
        [6] .... and I told her [7] .... She asked
        [8] .... and I said [9] .... and then she told me
        [10] .... Then I said ...

Peter: Now, hold on, Lucy! How did this fight start?

Lucy: Well, I can't remember now, but I will never forgive her! Well, not until after lunch, anyway ...

17 **Rewrite the sentences in direct speech.**

1 They wanted to know if I would return the books the following week.
   They asked me, 'Will you return the books next week?'

2 Keira asked me to make a sandwich. ....

3 The firefighter ordered us to stay back. ....

4 Mary said she would get up early the following day. ....

5 He said they were meeting their friends that day. ....

6 Jack said he had sent them an email the day before. ....

7 Nick told Tina she should be more careful in future. ....

8 Chris told me that he liked football. ....

9 Ian wondered where we were going that evening. ....

10 Ron wanted to know where my brother was. ....

Writing practice

18 **Read the interview and write a short article for *TeenLink*.**

TeenLink

You:	¹ Ms Jackson, what happened last Tuesday?
Ms Jackson:	² I wasn't feeling very well. ³ Then I fainted in the bathroom.
You:	⁴ Who called for help?
Ms Jackson:	⁵ It was Lucky, my golden retriever. ⁶ I live alone so I have trained Lucky to push the speed dial button for my sister's number on the telephone.
You:	⁷ Is it easy to train a dog to do this?
Ms Jackson:	⁸ Well, Lucky is a very clever dog so it was easy with him. ⁹ After what happened, two of my neighbours asked me to train their dogs, too. ¹⁰ I guess I'll answer your question in a few weeks!

A `Lucky´ escape!   by ....

Ms Jackson had a stroke of luck when she fell ill in her house a week ago - from none other than her dog, Lucky. I interviewed her at the park, while she was walking him.

At first, I asked Ms Jackson ¹ *what had happened the previous Tuesday* ....

She told ² *me that* ....

and that ³ ....

I asked ⁴ ....

and she said ⁵ ....

She added ⁶ ....

I wanted to know ⁷ ....

Ms Jackson ⁸ ....

She added ⁹ ....

so she ¹⁰ ....

Question tags, short agreements

Positive and negative forms; *'so'* / *'neither'* / *'nor'* ...

Harry: I'm hungry.

Peter: So am I. Let's go to that new burger place, shall we?

Lucy: Great. I'm coming with you!

Peter: We want to go alone, Lucy! Besides, you haven't finished your homework yet, have you?

Lucy: But Peter ...

Peter: I said no!

Erm ... Peter, I haven't got much money left ...

Neither have I. Let me think ...

On second thoughts, I really can't go and leave my little sister behind, can I?

You're not getting a penny out of me, Peter Hardy!

1 **Complete the tables.**

Question tags	
He is twelve years old, isn't ....?	She doesn't live in Pont Street, does she?
I'm doing the best I can, aren't I?	They didn't give you a key, ... they?
You have had dinner, ... you?	It wasn't going fast, was it?
They have been walking, haven't they?	The man hadn't left, had ....?
We'd finished by that time, ... we?	She won't answer the phone, will she?
She can't play chess, can she?	We mustn't leave now, must we?
Give me your pen, will you?	Let's not fight, shall we?

Short agreements

Statement	Agreement
I'm hungry.	So am I.
I'm not tired.	Neither / Nor am ....
I play basketball for the school team.	.... do I.
She doesn't know Tom.	Neither / Nor .... he.
They're doing a project.	So are we.
He hasn't seen the film.	.... / Nor have we.

2 **Read the information.**

Question tags
Use
We use a question tag at the end of a sentence when we are almost certain about something, but we would like our listener to confirm it.

Form
We form question tags with an auxiliary verb and a pronoun.
We always use a comma before a question tag.
Tom and Sandra go to school by bus, don't they?
Fred's got a baby sister, hasn't he?
They can't do this, can they?
• When the sentence is positive, the question tag is negative.
It's a lovely day, isn't it?
• When the sentence is negative, the question tag is positive.
Peter hasn't called, has he?

• When there is a negative word in the sentence (e.g. *never, rarely, seldom*), the question tag is positive.
She's never been to Italy, has she?
They seldom go out, do they?
• The question tag for *I am* is *aren't I?*
I'm lucky today, aren't I?
• The question tag for *Let's* is *shall we?* It is the same for positive and negative sentences.
Let's have a break, shall we?
Let's not go out tonight, shall we?
• The question tag for the imperative is *will you?* It is the same for positive and negative sentences.
Take these papers to Mr Smith, will you?
Don't make so much noise, will you?
• When the subject of a sentence is the word *there* (e.g. *There is / There are*) we also use it in the question tag, instead of a pronoun.
There's a big tree outside your house, isn't there?

3 **Circle the correct answer.**

1 Jen and Anna are staying at their aunt's, (aren't they) / isn't she?
2 He mustn't leave before he finishes, doesn't / must he?
3 You don't believe me, don't / do you?
4 They haven't invited us to the wedding, do / have they?
5 I'm telling the truth, am I not / aren't I?
6 There will be a pool at the hotel, won't there / it?
7 Let's talk about this another time, shall / won't we?
8 Don't shout, will / do you?
9 Your sister never wears jeans, doesn't / does she?
10 The owners of the shop weren't there, were they / was it?
11 Open the window for me, don't / will you?
12 Paul had been talking on the phone, had / hadn't he?
13 They had to think of a new plan, didn't / hadn't they?
14 We won't be ready tomorrow, will / shall we?

4 **Complete with a question tag.**

1 She won't go to school tomorrow, _will she_ ?
2 Look after your baby sister, ... ?
3 Let's play another game, ... ?
4 Nick doesn't mind waiting, ... ?
5 You were talking to Peter, ... ?
6 He rarely goes out for dinner, ... ?

7 They haven't packed their suitcase, yet, ... ?
8 I'm too early, ... ?
9 She never complains, ... ?
10 They won't be there when we arrive, ... ?
11 They couldn't stay here, ... ?
12 You've heard about him, ... ?

5 **Complete the questions with question tags. Then answer the questions and find your score.**

> ### Right or Wrong?
> **Kevin McMann's General knowledge TV quiz**
>
> **Kevin:** [1] Man walked on the moon for the first time in 1999, _didn't he_ ?
> **You:** Right / Wrong
>
> **Kevin:** [2] You'll find the 'Mona Lisa' in the Louvre, ... ?
> **You:** ....
>
> **Kevin:** [3] The next Olympic Games will be in Greece, ... ?
> **You:** ....
>
> **Kevin:** [4] Ice skating isn't an Olympic sport, ... ?
> **You:** ....
>
> **Kevin:** [5] Pandas live in Africa, ... ?
> **You:** ....
>
> **Kevin:** [6] Dolphins lay eggs, ... ?
> **You:** ....
>
> **Kevin:** [7] Cats can see in the dark, ... ?
> **You:** ....
>
> **Kevin:** [8] An iguana is a fish, ... ?
> **You:** ....
>
> **Kevin:** [9] Pierce Brosnan has appeared as James Bond in four films, ... ?
> **You:** ....
>
> **Kevin:** [10] William Shakespeare wrote 'Hamlet', ... ?
> **You:** ....
>
> Answers:
> 1 Wrong 2 Right 3 Wrong 4 Wrong 5 Wrong
> 6 Wrong 7 Right 8 Wrong 9 Right 10 Right

6 **Read the information.**

> **Short agreements**
> We use short agreements to agree with what someone has just said.
> • To agree with a positive statement we use
>   *So + auxiliary verb / modal + subject.*
> *I'm glad we are here.*
> *So am I.*
> *Sandra has bought this dress.*
> *So has my sister.*
>
> • To agree with a negative statement we use
>   *Neither / Nor + auxiliary verb / modal + subject.*
> *I don't like this place.*
> *Neither / Nor do I.*
> *They haven't got time.*
> *Neither / Nor have we.*

7 **Circle the correct answer.**

1 I can't sleep with the lights on. — (Neither can I) / So can't I.
2 He will appear in the school play. — So will I / So am I.
3 They haven't got their order yet. — Nor have we / Nor we have.
4 My mum likes getting up early. — So does mine / So my mum does.
5 They should ask permission. — So do you / So should you.
6 I didn't do any homework on Friday. — Nor did John / So did John.
7 We had dinner at 'Mario's' last week. — So had we / So did we.
8 I'm not going in there. — So am I / Neither am I.
9 Ellie doesn't know how to ski. — So do I / Neither do I.
10 We were cooking when the lights went out. — So were we / So did we.

8 **Complete with a short agreement.**

1 Paul works in a bank. ...*So does*.... Leo.
2 We hadn't seen a lion before. .... we.
3 We have enjoyed being here. .... we.
4 I read the whole book in one weekend. .... my sister.
5 Ben wasn't paying attention. .... you!

6 She doesn't know what to do. .... her friend.
7 I won't have anything to drink. .... I.
8 They must be more careful. .... we.
9 She isn't going to help us. .... he.
10 We may finish earlier tonight. .... I.

9 **Read and complete.**

Sophie: I'm really looking forward to the summer holidays!
Lucy: So [1] ...*am*... I.
Sophie: I want to do something different this time, [2] ...*don't*... you? I don't want to do the same things again and again.
Lucy: [3] .... do I.
Sophie: I'd like to go to summer camp, [4] .... you?
Lucy: No, we've been to summer camp, [5] .... we ? How about Africa? I want to go on safari!
Sophie: Oh, yes, [6] .... do I. You've never been to Africa before, [7] .... you?
Lucy: No, but I've seen documentaries on TV. It looks so exciting, [8] .... it?
Sophie: Yes, it does … (sigh)
Lucy: Or how about America? I'd love to go to Disneyland!
Sophie: So [9] .... I.
Lucy: Well, it doesn't hurt to dream, [10] .... it?
Sophie: I guess not …

10 **Write what you would say in these situations.**

1 Your friend has promised to buy tickets for a concert. You want to check that he / she is going to do it tomorrow. *You're going to buy the tickets tomorrow, aren't you?*
2 Your friend says 'I don't like snakes.' You agree. *Neither do I.*
3 You think your aunt has changed the colour of her hair. You ask her just to check if you are right.
....
4 Someone you've just met says: 'I think we've met before.' That's what you think, too.
....
5 Your mum says: 'I haven't had any breakfast, yet.' You haven't had any breakfast, either.
....

119

17 Defining and non-defining relative clauses

Relative clauses, clauses of purpose, result, reason, concession and contrast

TeenLink

When Lightning Strikes ...
by Harry Davis

Although we don't expect them, thunderstorms are quite common in spring and summer. Despite lasting a short time, thunderstorms are dangerous because they produce lightning, which can kill.

If you see lightning, which is a flash of light, and can hear thunder, which is a loud rumbling noise, you are so close to the storm that you might be in danger. Go to a safe place immediately, such as a house or a car. Whatever you do, don't stand under a tree. Trees attract lightning and it is not safe to shelter under them because of this.

Don't use the telephone or anything electrical because if lightning hits, it can travel through the electrical wires. It can travel through water, too, so don't take a bath or a shower. Swimming in the sea is also dangerous.

1 Complete the tables.

Defining relative clauses	
who / that	The young man who / .... spoke to me was Brian Williams. The girl (................ / that) you are talking about is my sister.
which / that	The dog which / .... appears in the advert belongs to my friend. The house (................ / that) they've bought used to be a gallery.
whose	The girl .... turn had come for an audition said she wasn't ready.
where	This is the spot .... we should plant the tree.
when	December is the month .... the shop is busiest.

Non-defining relative clauses	
who	Frank Campbell, ... directed the film, will not be there for the premiere.
which	This portrait, ... was painted by Henri Matisse, belonged to my great-grandmother.
whose	Mr Smith, ... son was getting married, invited us to the wedding.
where	She's going to visit Glasgow, ... she has relatives.
when	They moved house in 2001, ... their baby was born.

2 **Read the information.**

Relative clauses

We use relative clauses to give more information about a noun in the main sentence.

The man answered the phone. (main clause)
The man was my dad.
(information about the subject of the main clause)
The man who answered the phone was my dad.
(relative clause)

Relative pronouns

We use relative pronouns in the beginning of a relative clause. Relative pronouns refer to a noun in the main sentence and they come directly after it. Here's a list of relative pronouns:

- *who* for people
- *whom* for people
- *which* for things or animals
- *that* for people, animals or things
- *whose* for people, animals or things
- *where* for places
- *when* for time

The customer who bought the TV left his credit card behind.
The house which had stood at the top of the cliff was gone.
The town where I grew up is very small.

Defining relative clauses

Defining relative clauses give essential information about the noun they refer to. Without them, the main clause doesn't make sense. Look at the example:
The people are very noisy. (main sentence)
They live in the flat above ours.
(essential information)
The main clause doesn't make sense unless we define who we are talking about.
This information comes in the relative clause.
The people who live in the flat above us are very noisy.

- We place a defining relative clause directly after the noun it defines, without using a comma to separate them.

The woman who had found the lost cat was happy to return it to its owner.

- When we speak we prefer to use *that* instead of *who* or *which*.

What's the title of the song that is playing now?

- When the relative pronoun (*whom, which, that*) is the object of the relative clause, we usually leave it out.

The book is very good. (main clause)
You gave me this book. (*this book* is the object)
The book (that) you gave me is very good.

- We never leave out the relative pronoun if it refers to the subject of the main clause.

The book is very good. (main clause)
The book won the prize. (*the book* is the subject)
The book that won the prize is very good.

Non-defining relative clauses

- Non-defining relative clauses give us extra information about the noun to which they refer. The information is not essential because the main clause is complete without it.

Tom Davis is a well-known writer. (main clause)
Tom Davis is Harry's uncle.
(extra information about the subject of the main clause)
Tom Davis, who is Harry's uncle, is a well-known writer.

- We place a non-defining relative clause directly after the noun it defines. We use commas to separate the non-defining clause from the main clause.
- We never leave out the relative pronoun in a non-defining relative clause.
- We don't use the relative pronoun *that* in non-defining relative clauses.

Mr Brown's car, which was parked illegally, was taken away.
Sandra, whom you met last night, is a doctor.

3 Complete with a relative pronoun. If you have two options, write both of them.

1 Did you eat the cake .....which / that.......... was on the table?

2 Steven, ... had never been to the zoo before, was delighted.

3 The teacher introduced us to the new student, ... we had already met.

4 Mary's wearing the dress .... I bought for her for her birthday.

5 The man .... luggage had been lost made a complaint to the airline.

6 Is this the house .... Charles Dickens lived?

7 The woman .... spoke to me was very rude!

8 That was the day .... Oliver got his driver's licence.

9 PJ Rivo, ... real name is John Smith, stars in a new film.

10 Manchester is the town .... most of Ian's family live.

4 Cross out the relative pronoun where it can be omitted.

1 The printer ~~which~~ I bought last month has broken down.

2 I'm reading the book which you gave me.

3 The man who plays the electric guitar in this group is my cousin.

4 The woman whose bag had been stolen went to the police.

5 In the safari park, the lion that was nearest to our car tried to jump on it.

6 A man whom I had never seen before was sitting in my kitchen.

7 George knows someone who can help us.

8 The T-shirt that he's wearing is mine.

9 Is this the boy whose brother won the competition?

10 The girl that he has brought with him is a relative.

> **Look!**
>
> **Whose** is never omitted from the relative clause.

5 Join the sentences. Make the second sentence a defining relative clause.

1 The pizza is great. You have made the pizza.
The pizza (which / that) you have made is great.

2 The people were friendly. They've moved next door to us.
....

3 I know a girl. Her father is a professional footballer.
....

4 The man is Jenny's coach. He was talking to my dad.
....

5 The day finally came. Brian learned how to use the Internet.
....

6 The cottage was very comfortable. We spent our holidays there.
....

7 The phone number is wrong. William gave it to me.
....

8 This is the CD. I was telling you about it.
....

6 Read and put commas where necessary.

1 The man who delivered the parcel asked me to sign for it.

2 Samantha who had taken French lessons for two years could speak the language much better than us.

3 That's the building where my dad works.

4 Their garden which I can see from my bedroom window is the prettiest in the neighbourhood.

5 Kenneth who knew the area very well gave us directions.

6 Have you seen the book that Ron gave me?

7 Early in the morning when everyone is still asleep Mary gets up and takes the dog for a walk.

> **Look!**
>
> To decide if a relative clause is defining or non-defining, read the main clause on its own. If it makes sense, then the relative clause is non-defining. If you think some information is missing, or it doesn't make sense, then the relative clause is defining.

7 **Join the sentences. Make the second sentence a non-defining relative clause.**

1 There are two chairs in the garden shed. You can use them if you like.
   There are two chairs in the garden shed, which you can use if you like.

2 Paul looked very scruffy. He was wearing an old T-shirt and shorts.
   ....

3 The little girl smiled at me. I had just met her grandmother.
   ....

4 My aunt has a pony, two dogs and three cats. She lives in Cornwall.
   ....

5 Edinburgh is a beautiful city. I was born there.
   ....

6 The café was by the sea. It had a lovely view.
   ....

7 The school concert was a success. It was organised by the two music teachers.
   ....

8 Fred can speak fluent Spanish. He lived in Madrid for five years.
   ....

9 2004 was a lucky year for him. He won the lottery then.
   ....

10 Her new album isn't as good as the last one. It came out a few days ago.
   ....

8 **Join the sentences. Make the second sentence a defining or non-defining relative clause.**

TeenLink

Your questions answered!

What's wakeboarding?
Jess, 11

1 Wakeboarding, which is a water sport, is a combination of water–skiing and surfing.

What's a herbivore?
Timothy, 10

2 .... Just so that you know, 3 .... and 4 ....

How did the Dead Sea get its name?
Marianne, 12

5 ....
6 ....

If there is no kind of life then it is a 'dead' sea. That's how it got its name.

I've often heard of safari parks, but what are they exactly?
Jon, 11 and a half

7 ....

Visitors can drive their cars along special roads to see them.

8 .... It is not wise to get out of the safety of their car!

1 Wakeboarding is a combination of water ski-ing and surfing. It is a water sport.
2 A herbivore is an animal. It only eats plants.
3 A carnivore is an animal. It eats only meat.
4 A omnivore is an animal. It eats plants and meat.
5 The Dead Sea has 30% salt in its water. It is really a lake.
6 The Dead Sea has no plants or animals. They can't live in such salty waters.
7 A safari park is an area. Animals are kept in their natural environment.
8 People should be careful, though. They want to take photographs.

123

9 Complete the tables.

Clauses of purpose, result, reason, concession, contrast

Clauses of purpose

to	I've bought some apples .... make an apple pie.
in order to	I've bought some apples in .... to make an apple pie.
so that	I've bought some apples .... that we can make an apple pie.

Clauses of result

so	The day was hot, ... they decided to go for a swim.
so... that	The day was .... hot that they decided to go for a swim.
such... that	It was such a hot day .... they decided to go for a swim.

Clauses of reason

| *because* | The concert was cancelled .... there was a thunderstorm. |
| *because of* | The concert was cancelled because .... the thunderstorm. |

Clauses of concession

but	I felt tired, ... I decided to go to my cousin's party.
however	I felt tired. ...., I decided to go to my cousin's party.
although	.... I felt tired, I decided to go to my cousin's party.
in spite of	.... spite of feeling tired, I decided to go to my cousin's party.
despite	.... feeling tired, I decided to go to my cousin's party.

Clauses of contrast

| *while* | Tom is very energetic, ... Sam likes to do things slowly. |
| *whereas* | Tom is very energetic, ... Sam likes to do things slowly. |

10 Read the information.

Clauses of purpose

We use a clause of purpose when we want to state the purpose of the action in the main clause.

There are three different ways to form a clause of purpose

- *to* + infinitive

He hired an assistant to help him at the shop.

- *in order to* + infinitive

They went to the bank in order to see the manager.

- *so that* + subject + *can / will* (for the present)

I'll leave early so that I won't need to rush.

- *so that* + subject + *could / would* (for the past)

She finished her homework quickly so that she could watch her favourite TV show.

Clauses of result

We use a clause of result when we talk about the result that comes from the main clause.

There are three ways to form a clause of result

- *so* + clause

We missed the last bus so we had to take a cab.

- *so* + adjective/adverb + *that*

The film was so good that I saw it twice.

- *such* + *a / an* + adjective + singular noun + *that*

It was such an interesting book that I couldn't put it down.

- *such* + adjective + plural noun / uncountable noun + *that*

They were such well-behaved kids that everyone loved them.

Clauses of reason

We use a clause of reason when we want to talk about why something in the main clause happens.

There are two different ways to form a clause of reason

- *because* + clause

We are happy because we've just had some good news.

- *because of* + noun

Our flight was cancelled because of the fog.

Clauses of concession

We use these when we want to show that what the main clause states happens in spite of what the clause of concession states.

There are four different ways to form a clause of concession

- *but* + clause

I tried to call her but her mobile was switched off.

- *However,* + clause

John hated beans. However, he ate the bean soup without a word.

- *although* + clause

Although we were late, she refused to hurry.

- *in spite of / despite* + gerund

There is no difference in meaning or use between *in spite of* and *despite*.

In spite of following the instructions, we couldn't make the machine work.

Despite playing well, he lost the game.

- *in spite of / despite* + the fact that + clause

In spite of the fact that they knew no one at the party, they had a good time.

- *in spite of / despite* + noun

The climbers started early in the morning despite the bad weather forecast.

Clauses of contrast

We use these when we want to show that what the clause of contrast states is the opposite of what the main clause states.

There are two different ways to form a clause of contrast

- *while* + clause

You are a good singer while I am dreadful!

- *whereas* + clause

These shoes are expensive whereas those shoes are more reasonably priced.

---

11 **Choose the correct answer.**

1   I'm saving money so that / (in order to) buy a new MP3 player.

2   He asked me to / in order help him so that he would finish on time.

3   They flew to New York so that / to see their son who is studying there.

4   I gave Mary my sweater so that / to she could keep warm.

5   In order / So that to apply for a driving licence you have to be eighteen years old.

6   Grandad's learning how to send emails in order to / so that he can write to his grandchildren.

7   They took a camera with them to / so that take some photos.

8   You must label your things in order / so that we'll know they are yours.

9   He has to go to the shops so / in order to get new trainers.

10   Ben gets up early so that / in order to he can exercise before work.

12 Join the sentences using the words given.

1 I put all the cans in a bag. I wanted to take them to the recycling bin.   **to**
   I put all the cans in a bag to take them to the recycling bin.

2 Paul bought some snacks. He wanted to treat his friends.   **in order to**

3 She ran as fast as she could. She wanted to catch the bus.   **in order to**

4 I phone my granny every week. I want to see how she's doing.   **to**

5 Mary is going to London. She wants to see an exhibition.   **in order to**

6 They are revising the whole book. They want to do well in the test.   **in order to**

7 They sent me an email. They wanted to invite me to their house.   **to**

8 I put on a hat. I wanted to protect my face from the sun.   **to**

13 Rewrite the sentences using *so that*.

1 She always packs her school bag in the evening in order to get more sleep in the morning.
   She always packs her school bag in the evening so that she can get more sleep in the morning.

2 I bought a newspaper to have something to read on the bus.

3 Jane left early in order to go to the doctor.

4 She exercises every day to get fitter.

5 They leave the window open in order to get some fresh air.

6 He set the alarm clock to wake up early the following day.

> **Look!**
>
> Remember: *so* + adjective/adverb + *that*
> *such* + *a* + adjective + singular noun
> *such* + adjective + plural noun
> *such* + adjective + uncountable noun

14 Join the sentences.

1 Diana is an interesting speaker. I can listen to her for hours.
   Diana is such *an interesting speaker that I can listen to her for hours.*

2 It was a small car. It could only take two people.
   The car was so ....

3 The flowers were beautiful. I didn't want to cut them.
   They were such ....

4 The news is exciting. I can't keep it to myself.
   It is such ....

5 He is a very good friend. I would do anything for him.
   He is such ....

6 The party finished late. I fell asleep in the car on the way home.
   The party finished so ....

7 The books were valuable. We had to wear white gloves to touch them.
   They were such ....

Look!

Read the sentences first and decide which of the two talks about the result.

15 **Join the sentences using *so*.**

1 George is thrilled. His team has just won the Cup. *George's team has just won the Cup, so he is thrilled.*
2 There is a sale. You can buy things at a reduced price. ....
3 I am going home. I've got lots of homework to do. ....
4 You can have the coffee machine. We don't use it. ....
5 She called her dad. She wanted to ask him something. ....
6 The school bus was late today. I missed the first lesson. ....
7 They knew they were wrong. They apologised. ....
8 I know all their lyrics. I listen to their CDs all the time. ....

16 **Complete with *because* or *because of*.**

1 They were tired ..*because*.... they had been playing all day.
2 The road was closed .... the accident that had happened earlier.
3 She didn't watch the film to the end .... she didn't like it.
4 I can't remember the details .... it has been ages since I read it.
5 We couldn't sit outside .... the wind.
6 He took an umbrella with him .... it was going to rain.
7 I had to miss the school trip .... my broken leg.
8 They hadn't heard anything I'd said .... the noise.

Look!

Remember:
because + clause
because of + noun

17 **Read, choose and complete.**

however (x2)   although   despite (x2)   but   spite

TeenLink

How to protect yourself ...

Shark Attack!

If you see a shark while you're swimming, first of all try to stay calm. ¹ ..*Despite*..... the urge to start splashing about and shouting for help, try to swim away from it as smoothly and as fast as you can. Don't even think of attacking it first. ² ...., if the shark attacks, the best thing you can do is hit it. You might think that 'playing dead' is better ³ .... it really won't help.

⁴ .... some people advise hitting the shark on the nose, the best place to hit it is between the eyes. Using a stick or a pole to do so is best because this will also keep you away from the shark. ⁵ ...., since people do not usually swim carrying sticks or poles, you can use your fist or fingers to poke at it.

In ⁶ .... of the belief that sharks like to attack people, they usually think they're attacking a big fish. Also, ⁷ .... the popular myth that all sharks are dangerous, you will be relieved to know that almost 80% of all shark species are completely harmless for humans.

18 **Rewrite the sentences using the words given.**

1 She is very tall. However, they didn't offer her a place in the school basketball team. **despite**
Despite the fact that she's very tall, they didn't offer her a place in the school basketball team.

2 The new table arrived, but the chairs didn't. **although**

3 Although they are twins they don't look the same. **however**

4 In spite of taking cookery lessons, she is still an awful cook. **although**

5 He is a good actor, but he didn't get the part in the film. **in spite of**

6 Although it was a difficult thing to do, they succeeded. **but**

7 We ran to the station, but when we got there the train had already left. **however**

8 Although he works in the city, he has chosen to live in the country. **in spite of**

9 Despite the fact that he seems friendly, I don't really like him. **but**

10 Although the film was a comedy, no-one laughed. **despite**

19 **Join the sentences with *and* or *while / whereas.***

1 January is a cold month in Europe. In Australia it is a hot month.
January is a cold month in Europe, whereas in Australia it is a hot month.

2 She has a good voice. She plays the piano very well.

3 I love romantic films. My brother thinks they're silly.

4 It has been a long time since we last met. He won't remember me.

5 We wanted to play football. They wanted to go skating.

6 They usually spend their holidays in the mountains. We prefer the sea.

7 We found some eggs in the fridge. We made an omelette.

8 I try to have a healthy diet. He only eats junk food.

9 You were very helpful. Your colleague was very rude.

10 I realised I was wrong. I apologised to my friend.

> **Look!**
>
> We use *and* to join sentences that talk about similar things. We use *while / whereas* to join sentences that talk about opposite things.

20 **Read and complete. Use only *one* word.**

TeenLink

My Favourite Tale ...
My granny used to tell me this story when I was younger and I loved it!
Emma Johnson, 13

The Sun and the Wind
One day, the Sun and the Wind, had a disagreement. The Wind said that he was stronger than the Sun ¹ ..*because*.... he could blow anything he wanted away. ² .... the Sun insisted that he ruled everything on Earth and no one had more power than he did. The Wind, ³ .... was really annoyed with the Sun, said: 'Let's have a competition to see who's right!' It pointed to an old shepherd, ⁴ .... sheep were grazing on a field right below them. The shepherd was wearing a coat ⁵ .... looked thick and heavy. 'I bet you I can blow ⁶ .... hard ⁷ .... I'll take the coat right off the old man's back,' the Wind said. The Sun smiled. 'I think that competitions are a waste of time. ⁸ ...., I'll take part in this just to prove how wrong you are.' The Wind frowned, took a deep breath and began to blow ...

(The story continues in exercise 21.)

Writing practice

21 **Join the sentences using the word given to finish the story.**

1 The Wind blew as hard as it could. The shepherd pulled his coat around him tightly.   **however**
2 He tied it round his waist with a piece of string. He was cold.   **because**
3 The Wind had done its best. It hadn't been able to blow the man's coat away.   **although**
4 The Sun smiled. The Wind cried with anger, 'Well, if I can't do it, neither can you!'   **while**
5 The Sun turned its head. It wanted to face the Earth.   **in order to**
6 It shone brightly. The old shepherd felt hot and took off his heavy coat.   **so ... that**

The Wind blew as hard as he could. However, the shepherd pulled his coat around him tightly.

Prepositions

Prepositions of time, place and movement,
dependent prepositions, phrasal verbs

'HELP!'

1 **Read the table.**

Prepositions of time	We're going to Paul's on Friday. I need to get up early in the morning.
Prepositions of place	There's a café next to the bookshop. Your bag is behind that chair.
Prepositions of movement	The students ran out of the classroom. He climbed down the ladder.
Adjective-dependent prepositions	This T-shirt is different from Mary's. Are you interested in yoga?
Verb-dependent prepositions	You must apologise for what you have done. I don't agree with what he is saying.
Phrasal verbs	We've just run out of juice. Why do they keep putting off their visit?

2 **Read the information**

Prepositions of time

at

We use *at* with

* the time: *at half past three, at 2 p.m.*
* the expressions: *at the moment, at present, at night, at noon / midday / midnight, at lunch(time) / dinner(time), at the weekend, at Christmas, at Easter*

on

We use *on*

* with days of the week: *on Tuesday, on Sunday*
* with (day) + morning / afternoon / evening: *on Wednesday morning, on Saturday evening*
* with dates: *on 25th July*

* whenever a specific day is mentioned: *on Christmas Day / Boxing Day, on New Year's Day / Eve, on her birthday, on their wedding day, on that day, on the day, on a warm day etc*

in

We use *in* with

* centuries: *in the 16th century, in the 21st century*
* years: *in 1865, in 2008*
* seasons: *in (the) spring / summer / autumn / winter*
* months: *in June, in October*
* these expressions: *in the morning / afternoon / evening*

3 **Complete with *at, on* or *in*.**

1 The film finished ...*at*........... midnight.
2 I'll see you .... 5 o'clock tomorrow.
3 .... New Year's Eve there was a firework display.
4 The office will be closed .... 27th December.
5 What clothes did they use to wear .... the 17th century?

6 Oliver is leaving .... Saturday.
7 They usually eat out .... weekends.
8 .... winter, most birds fly south.
9 Are you doing anything .... Saturday morning?
10 My birthday's .... the 1st of August.
11 Her sister was born .... 2001.
12 .... summer evenings we eat on the balcony.

4 **Read the information**

Prepositions of place

The most common prepositions of place are:

at:	John's at work.
in:	The money is in my bag.
inside:	Open the box and have a look inside.
outside:	The children are playing outside.
on:	There's a plate on the table.
over:	The tree branch is hanging over the roof.
above:	He lives in a flat above his shop.
under:	We sat under the shade of a tree.
below:	The temperature had dropped to 10 degrees below zero.
in front of:	I couldn't see because there were two tall men in front of me.
behind:	The little boy hid behind the sofa so that his friend wouldn't see him.
near:	The supermarket is near our house.
next to:	Susan sits next to me in class.
beside:	Come and sit beside me.
opposite:	Jane sat opposite Nick at the table so that they could talk.
between:	There's a painting between the door and the window.
among:	I could easily recognise him among other people.

With the following expressions we use these prepositions:

at home, at school, at work, on the chair, in the armchair, on the left, on the right, in bed, in hospital, in prison, in the city, in town
in + town / city: in London
at + address: at 12 Castle Street
in + street: in Oxford Street

5 **Read the information.**

Prepositions of movement

We use prepositions of movement together with verbs of movement to show the direction in which someone or something moves. The prepositions of movement are:

to	He went to the kitchen and made some tea.
from	I ran all the way from school to his house.
towards	They started to walk towards the car but someone stopped them.
up	I climbed up the stairs to the third floor.
down	We sat down.
onto	The cat jumped onto the sofa.
off	Take your feet off the desk!
over	The captain informed us that we were flying over the Alps.
into	As soon as it started to rain everyone ran into the house.
out of	He took a rabbit out of his hat.
round	As I went round the corner, I saw the side door.
along	Come along with us. We're going to have a great time!
across	We walked across the river at its most shallow point.
past	I go past this shop every day on my way to work.
through	To go to the back of the house we had to go through the living room.

Which preposition?

to, towards
She went to the corner shop.
(she arrived there)
She went towards the shop.
(that's the direction she took – we don't know if she's arrived or not)

on, onto
John is on his bike.
(we use on when something is stationary)
John climbed onto his bike and left.
(we use onto with movement)

in, inside, into
The toothbrushes are in / inside the cabinet.
(we use in / inside when something is stationary)
I put the toothbrushes into the cabinet.
(we use into with movement)

over, above
The book is on the shelf over / above the desk.
(both are correct when something is stationary)
The bird flew over our heads.
(we use over with movement)

beside, next to
The sugar is beside / next to the coffee.
(they have the same meaning)

under, below
Your shoes are under the bed.
We flew so high that the clouds were below us.
His paintings aren't good – in fact they're below average.
(below means lower than a certain level)

between, among
In the photo I'm the one between my uncle and my dad.
(when there are two people, things etc)
She was the best among her classmates.
(when there are more than two people, things etc)

on, off
We put the PC on the desk.
We took the PC off the desk because it took up too much space.
(off is the opposite of on – it means 'to remove')

6 Circle the correct answer.

1 Martha has lived at /(in) London all her life.
2 I went towards / to the supermarket yesterday so the fridge is well-stocked.
3 Why don't we walk to / at the sports centre? That's exercise, too!
4 The hamster ran into / in the corner so we were able to catch it.
5 It's going to rain. Let's put the chairs inside / outside.
6 Adrian walked past / through the shop every day, but he had never noticed it.
7 Look, John's the one sitting between / among Chris and my brother.
8 Oliver ran across / over the road to say hello to us.
9 The garden door was locked so I had to climb above / over the fence to get in.
10 Were you at / in home yesterday?
11 Diana came and sat behind / beside me so that we could talk.
12 The museum café is at the level under / below this one.
13 I left a note for Mum onto / on the kitchen table saying we wouldn't be late.
14 They live in / at 2 Thames Terrace, SW1.
15 Sit in / on this chair. It's more comfortable than that one.
16 I saw Ben as he was coming off / out of the post office.

7 Read the information.

> **Dependent prepositions**
>
> There are some set expressions that involve the use of specific prepositions with certain words. These combinations are: adjective + preposition or verb + preposition.
>
> **Adjective-dependent prepositions**
> Here's a list of the most common combinations of adjectives and prepositions:
>
> | | |
> |---|---|
> | addicted to | fond of |
> | afraid of | interested in |
> | angry about (something) | jealous of |
> | angry with (somebody) | keen on |
> | annoyed with | made of |
> | bad / good at | proud of |
> | bored with | ready for |
> | connected to | sad about |
> | crazy about | scared of |
> | dependent on | similar to |
> | different from | sorry about / for |
> | dressed in | the same as |
> | enthusiastic about | tired of |
> | fed up with | worried about |
>
> She looks different from her photo.
> I'm not very interested in skating.
>
> **Verb-dependent prepositions**
> Here's a list of the most common combinations of verbs and prepositions:
>
> | | |
> |---|---|
> | agree with | dream about |
> | allergic to | escape from |
> | apologise for | explain to |
> | apply for | hear from |
> | argue with | laugh at |
> | arrive at / in | lie about |
> | believe in | listen to |
> | belong to | pay for |
> | borrow from | reply to |
> | consist of | search for |
> | crash into | shout at |
> | depend on | take care of |
> | disagree with | wait for |
>
> Do you believe in ghosts?
> I agree with what he's just said.

8 **Circle the correct answer.**

1 I'm very angry with / (sorry for) shouting at you. I shouldn't have done it.
2 Who's proud of / interested in a game of Scrabble?
3 If you laugh at / shout at what I'm going to say, I will never speak to you again!
4 I'm fed up with / fond of doing the same things every weekend. I need a change!
5 You don't need to do anything. Elsie has consisted of / taken care of everything.
6 Kate is crazy about / fed up with this band – she's got all their CDs.
7 Has anyone heard from / crashed into Mark? He's been away for months!
8 Look! Your bag is the same as / connected to Jade's.
9 My sister's afraid of / worried about the dark so she sleeps with a light on.
10 Don't argue with / agree with your father. You know he is right.

9 **Circle the correct answer.**

1 They are worried ....*about*.... their granny, who is in hospital.
(a about)   b with   c after
2 You're very .... at drawing. Have you taken lessons?
a enthusiastic   b keen   c good
3 I never agree .... Ian. He and I are so different.
a about   b with   c for
4 She .... for her sandwich and mine.
a took care   b applied   c paid
5 We borrowed some glasses .... the neighbours.
a for   b from   c of
6 Is this fruit bowl made .... wood?
a of   b from   c for
7 By the time they .... at the village it was already dark.
a arrived   b escaped   c crashed

10 **Choose and complete.**

belong   keen   explain   similar   tired   ~~shouted~~   angry   proud

1 The coach ...*shouted*...at me because I wasn't fast enough. I felt awful!
2 She's very .... on vintage teddy bears. She's got a big collection.
3 This jacket must .... to you. It's got your name written on the inside.
4 I'm .... of waiting. I think I'll go home.
5 Diana was very .... with Gus because he had lied to her.
6 This exercise isn't too difficult. Let me .... it to you.
7 This dress is very .... to the one you're wearing. They're almost the same!
8 Mum is very .... of my brother. He got straight As in his last report.

11 **Complete with the correct preposition.**

1 She bought the tickets and waited outside the cinema ...*for*... her friend to arrive.
2 This sandwich is different .... the one I ordered.
3 He lied .... his age. He said he was fifteen whereas he was thirteen.
4 Are you ready .... the game?
5 He apologised .... being late.
6 Did you know that Adrian is scared .... mice?
7 I don't know if we'll go to the beach tomorrow. It depends .... the weather.

12 **Read and complete. Use only one word in each space.**

TeenLink

Get the Job!

For those of you who are leaving school or looking for a summer job, here's some useful advice from Ms Elaine Wood, who's a career guidance counsellor.

If you are keen [1] ...*on*........ making a good impression, you might want to consider the following:

When you apply [2] .... a job, never lie [3] .... what you can do. You will soon be found out.

    Take care over how you look for the interview. You should wear clean and tidy clothes.

    Arrive [4] .... the place of the interview ten minutes early. This will give you time to collect your thoughts before you go in.

    If you are late for some reason, apologise [5] .... being late.

    If there are other people waiting for an interview, wait [6] .... your turn patiently. Don't walk up and down the room, looking at your watch.

    When you go in for the interview you need to show that you are very interested [7] .... the job. Don't be afraid to ask questions if you have any.

    You don't have to agree [8] .... everything the interviewers say. They might think you don't have any opinions of your own! But you shouldn't argue [9] .... them, either.

    Listen [10] .... all the questions carefully and answer them clearly.

If the interviewers say that you'll hear [11] .... them, thank them and go [12] .... of the room. With a bit of luck, you'll get the job!

13 **Read the information**

Phrasal verbs

- Phrasal verbs consist of two or three words. One word is always a verb and the other (or others) is a preposition or an adverb.
- The meaning of the phrasal verb is usually very different from the meaning of the separate words that it consists of.
call off = cancel

They called off the game because of the bad weather.
  run out of = something finishes
I've run out of ink for my printer. I'll have to go and buy some.
- The verb part of the phrasal verb changes its form just like it does when it is used on its own.

4 **Circle the correct answer.**

1. They've known each other for a long time but I don't think they go / **get** on.
2. The car stopped because it had **gone / run out of** petrol.
3. I'm not feeling very well. I think I'll go and **lie / get** down.
4. Olga gave **away / up** all the clothes she didn't want to keep.
5. I've been looking **for / after** you all afternoon. Where have you been?
6. They looked **for / through** all the photos, but couldn't find the one they wanted.
7. David **turned / made** up after everyone else had gone home.
8. Don't let a silly thing like this get you **down / on**. Cheer up!
9. We're looking **after / forward to** my aunt's cats now that she's on holiday.
10. Can you please **pick / break** up the oranges that have fallen off the orange tree?

15 **Choose and complete.**

| look up to | put out | make for | set off | ~~go off~~ | take up | give up | go out |

1 I don't like the smell of the milk. I think it has ..*gone off*......

2 David has .... drinking coffee. He only drinks green tea now.

3 He turned round and .... of the door before I had chance to answer.

4 She admires her cousin and has always .... her.

5 I'd like to .... golf. Do you think it's the right sport for me?

6 This is where I keep the candles in case the lights .... at night.

7 Don't forget to .... the fire after you finish the barbecue.

8 If they want to be on time they need to .... earlier than 9 o'clock.

16 **Complete the phrasal verbs.**

1 She was carried ..*away*........ by his enthusiasm and agreed to help him.

2 They got .... at the wrong station so they had to wait for the next train.

3 The thief made .... with more than £30,000 in stolen goods.

4 They had to take .... their dirty shoes before they went into the house.

5 He was brought .... in a lovely little village by the sea.

6 Are you telling the truth or have you made .... this story?

7 Could you hold ....? There's someone on the other line.

8 I'm really looking .... to going on holiday next week!

9 They turned .... all the lights before they went to bed.

10 If you don't know what this word means, why don't you look it .... in the dictionary?

17 **Read and complete. Use only one word in each space.**

TeenLink

The Help! page

My best friend got two kittens as a present from her aunt ¹ ....*on*.......... her last birthday.
Evie (that's my friend's name) is crazy ² .... them. They sleep ³ .... her bed and
they are very friendly and playful. The thing is, I have never been keen ⁴ .... cats, but I now I
have discovered that I am allergic ⁵ .... them! I start to sneeze and my eyes water
whenever they come near me. I am annoyed ⁶ .... Evie, who does not take this seriously and
says that I'm just jealous ⁷ .... them! She really seems more interested ⁸ ....
her cats than me!
Lea, 12

First of all you should make your friend listen ⁹ .... you. You need to explain
¹⁰ .... her that an allergy is not something you can choose to have. But be careful not
to get carried ¹¹ .... and start a fight, though. Tell her that she needs to look
¹² .... your friendship in the same way as she takes ¹³ .... of her cats.
Then you must work ¹⁴ .... the technical stuff, like where you should meet so that you
don't have to come near the cats. I'm sure that once she realises there really is a problem she
will be glad to do something about it.

18 **Read and write.**

In what ways are teenagers similar or different from one another? Send your ideas to help Harry with his survey for *TeenLink*.

TeenLink

TeenLink **Survey**

Tell us who you are and help us write about teenagers today.

We'd like to know more about:

What you are crazy about.
Who or what you are fond of.
Who or what you are fed up with.
Who you look up to and who you are angry with.
What you usually lie about.
What you are afraid of and what fills you with hope.

Dear TeenLink,
Here are a few things about me. I hope they help.
I'm really crazy about ....
....
....
....
....
....
....
....
....
....
....
....
....
....

Use your English (Units 15–18)

1 **Read the dialogue and complete the paragraph.**

Peter: [1] I'm going to the sports centre to play basketball. [2] Do you want to come?

Harry: [3] I can't. [4] I have to finish my homework first.

Peter: [5] I haven't done my homework, yet. [6] I'll do it tonight.

Harry: [7] You're going to be too tired to do it later and [8] there's a football match on TV at 7 o'clock [9] You won't be able to watch it.

Peter: Yes, you're right. [10] I hadn't thought of that.

Harry: [11] Go home and do your homework now. [12] I'll come round to your house at 6.30 and we'll watch the match together.

Peter: Ok, ok. [13] Don't forget to bring some crisps! [14] We haven't got any at home.

When Harry opened the door, he saw Peter standing on the doorstep. Peter told Harry that
[1] *he was going to the sports centre to play basketball* and asked him [2] ....
Harry [3] .... because [4] .... Peter told Harry
[5] .... and that [6] .... Harry [7] .... and
[8] .... [9] .... Peter agreed with Harry and
[10] .... Finally, Harry [11] .... He also
[12] .... Before he left, Peter [13] .... because
[14] .... at home.

2 **Complete with a question tag.**

1 She's playing for the other team, *isn't she* ?
2 He won't be able to get tickets for the show, ... ?
3 Don't be late, ... ?
4 They had already read the book, ... ?
5 It rained last night, ... ?
6 Sam doesn't like pop music, ... ?
7 I'm going to be in trouble, ... ?
8 We haven't had a reply to our email, ...

3 **Join the sentences using a defining or non-defining relative clause.**

1 The woman is standing next to Mr Brown. She is his wife.
   The woman who is standing next to Mr Brown is his wife.

2 We visited the National Gallery. It was my favourite.
   We visited ....

3 This is the shop. I buy all my clothes here.
   This ....

4 You gave me some advice. It was very useful.
   The advice ....

5 Steven Travis is my dad's oldest friend. He is a film director.
   Steven Travis, ...

6 The time came at last. Tina could run again after the accident.
   The time ....

7 The man thanked me. His son was in my team.
   The man ....

8 Adele didn't want to go to bed so early. She had slept all afternoon.
   Adele, ...

4 **Rewrite the sentences using the word given.**

1 I took some money out of the bank so that I could do some shopping.
   I took .... some shopping. **order**

2 Although the problem wasn't difficult, no one solved it.
   The problem .... solved it. **but**

3 I'm terrible at skiing, while Betty is an expert.
   Betty .... awful. **whereas**

4 It was an expensive dress. However, it was very ugly.
   It was an ugly .... expensive. **despite**

5 The day had been so tiring that she couldn't keep her eyes open.
   It had been .... her eyes open. **such**

6 The game was cancelled because it rained heavily.
   The game .... heavy rain. **of**

5 **Complete with *one* word.**

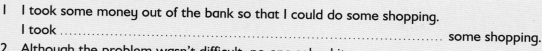

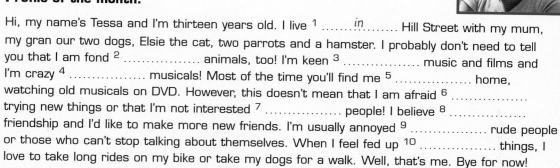

Look At You!
Profile of the month.

Hi, my name's Tessa and I'm thirteen years old. I live [1] ....*in*........ Hill Street with my mum, my gran our two dogs, Elsie the cat, two parrots and a hamster. I probably don't need to tell you that I am fond [2] .... animals, too! I'm keen [3] .... music and films and I'm crazy [4] .... musicals! Most of the time you'll find me [5] .... home, watching old musicals on DVD. However, this doesn't mean that I am afraid [6] .... trying new things or that I'm not interested [7] .... people! I believe [8] .... friendship and I'd like to make more new friends. I'm usually annoyed [9] .... rude people or those who can't stop talking about themselves. When I feel fed up [10] .... things, I love to take long rides on my bike or take my dogs for a walk. Well, that's me. Bye for now!

Now you can ...

✔ Report other people's words.
'I don't know his name.'
She said that she didn't know his name.
'Ann arrived yesterday.'
They told me that Ann had arrived the day before.

✔ Ask someone to confirm what you know.
He hasn't phoned yet, has he?
You play tennis, don't you?

✔ Agree with someone.
I'm happy to hear this.
So am I.
I don't like pizza.
Neither do I.

✔ Use relative clauses to give more information.
The woman who called didn't leave a message.
Diana, who was the first to finish the test, left early.

✔ Use clauses of purpose, result, reason, concession and contrast to express more complex ideas.
I left the door open so that the cat could come in.
In spite of the fact that he hated the opera, he decided to come with us.

✔ Use dependent prepositions appropriately.
I took the book off the shelf.
This T-shirt is different from the one you have.

Irregular Verbs

Infinitive	Past simple	Past participle
be	was/were	been
beat	beat	beaten
become	became	become
bend	bent	bent
begin	began	begun
bet	bet	bet
bite	bit	bitten
blow	blew	blown
break	broke	broken
bring	brought	brought
build	built	built
burn	burned/burnt	burned/burnt
buy	bought	bought
catch	caught	caught
choose	chose	chosen
come	came	come
cost	cost	cost
cut	cut	cut
dig	dug	dug
do	did	done
draw	drew	drawn
dream	dreamed/dreamt	dreamed/dreamt
drink	drank	drunk
drive	drove	driven
eat	ate	eaten
fall	fell	fallen
feed	fed	fed
feel	felt	felt
fight	fought	fought
find	found	found
fly	flew	flown
forget	forgot	forgotten
forgive	forgave	forgiven
freeze	froze	frozen
get	got	got
give	gave	given
go	went	gone
grow	grew	grown
hang	hung	hung
hear	heard	heard
have	had	had
hide	hid	hidden
hit	hit	hit
hold	held	held
hurt	hurt	hurt
keep	kept	kept
know	knew	known

Infinitive	Past simple	Past participle
lay	laid	laid
lead	led	led
learn	learned/learnt	learned/learnt
leave	left	left
lend	lent	lent
let	let	let
lie	lay	lain
lose	lost	lost
make	made	made
mean	meant	meant
meet	met	met
pay	paid	paid
put	put	put
read	read	read
ride	rode	ridden
ring	rang	rung
rise	rose	risen
run	ran	run
say	said	said
see	saw	seen
sell	sold	sold
send	sent	sent
set	set	set
shake	shook	shaken
shine	shone	shone
show	showed	shown
shut	shut	shut
sing	sang	sung
sit	sat	sat
sleep	slept	slept
smell	smelled/smelt	smelled/smelt
speak	spoke	spoken
spend	spent	spent
stand	stood	stood
steal	stole	stolen
swim	swam	swum
take	took	taken
teach	taught	taught
tell	told	told
think	thought	thought
throw	threw	thrown
understand	understood	understood
wake	woke	woken
wear	wore	worn
win	won	won
write	wrote	written

Spelling rules

Present simple

- To form the third person singular *(he, she, it)* of most verbs in the present simple, we add *-s*:
  walk ➜ walks
  ride ➜ rides
  sit ➜ sits
- We add *-es* to verbs that end in *-o, -ss, -ch, -sh* or *-x*:
  go ➜ goes   miss ➜ misses
  push ➜ pushes   match ➜ matches
  fix ➜ fixes
- For verbs that end in consonant + *-y*, we change *-y* to *-i* and add *-es*:
  study ➜ studies   try ➜ tries
but
- For verbs that end in vowel + *-y*, we just add *-s*:
  play ➜ plays   enjoy ➜ enjoys

Verb + *-ing*

- To make the *-ing* form of most verbs, we add *-ing* at the end of the verb:
  talk ➜ talking
  read ➜ reading
  say ➜ saying
- For verbs that end in *-e*, we take away the *-e* and add *-ing*:
  live ➜ living
  take ➜ taking
but
- For verbs that end in *-ee*, we add *-ing*:
  see ➜ seeing
  agree ➜ agreeing
- With one-syllable verbs that end in one vowel + consonant, we double the final consonant and add *-ing*:
  run ➜ running
  fit ➜ fitting
but
- For one-syllable verbs that end in two vowels + consonant, we just add *-ing*:
  eat ➜ eating
  cook ➜ cooking
  For two-syllable verbs that end in a vowel and consonant, we double the consonant if the stress is on the second syllable:
  begin ➜ beginning
but
  For two-syllable verbs that end in a vowel and consonant, we don't double the consonant if the stress is on the first syllable:
  shorten ➜ shortening

Past simple

- We add -ed to most regular verbs:
  look → looked   answer → answered   pull → pulled
- For verbs that end in -e we add -d:
  like → liked   dance → danced
- For verbs that end in consonant + -y, we change -y to -i and add -ed:
  cry → cried   study → studied

but

- For verbs that end in vowel + -y, we add -ed:
  play → played   stay → stayed
- For verbs that end in one vowel + consonant, we double the final consonant and add -ed:
  drop → dropped   fit → fitted

but

- For verbs that end in two vowels + consonant, we just add -ed:
  heat → heated   colour → coloured
- For verbs that end in -l, we double the last letter before we add -ed:
  travel → travelled   shovel → shovelled

Comparatives and superlatives

- To form the comparative and superlative of most one or two syllable adjectives, we add -er or -es
  fast → faster → the fastest
  young → younger → the youngest
  warm → warmer → the warmest
- For adjectives that end in -e, we add -r or -st:
  wise → wiser → the wisest
  late → later → the latest
- For one syllable adjectives that end in one vowel + consonant, we double the final consonant and
  add -er or -est:
  thin → thinner → the thinnest
  hot → hotter → (the) hottest
- For adjectives that end in -y, we change -y to -i and add -er or -est:
  healthy → healthier → the healthiest
  lazy → lazier → the laziest

Adverbs of manner

- To form most adverbs of manner, we add -ly to an adjective:
  polite → politely   careless → carelessly
- For adjectives that end in -y, we change -y to -i and add -ly:
  tidy → tidily   pretty → prettily   easy → easily
- For adjectives that end in -l, we add -ly:
  careful → carefully   beautiful → beautifully